Wicked Cripple Creek District

Jan MacKell Collins

THE
History
PRESS

Published by The History Press
Charleston, SC
www.historypress.com

First published 2024

Manufactured in the United States

ISBN 9781467157933

Library of Congress Control Number: 2024938200

CONTENTS

ACKNOWLEDGEMENTS

$\mathcal{H}$aving first visited the historic Cripple Creek District when I was but a child, living there for many years and continuing to keep this very special place close to my heart for some fifty years, I am indebted to numerous people, both living and not, who have helped me as I've followed a wild path, digging up as much history of the area as possible. They include, but are certainly not limited to, Steve Antonnucio and Dane Rhodes of Encore Video Productions; Burt, Mary and Norma Bielz; former *Sentinel* newspaper owner Al Born; my friend Boston; Krystal Brown; Charlotte Bumgarner of the Old Homestead House parlor house museum; Bill Burcaw and Jeanne Gripp of the Cripple Creek District Museum; Marlin, June and Melissa Bradley and Maria Conley; Rob Carrigan; Gus and Stanley Conley; Artie Crisp, Abigail Fleming, Samantha Linnane and the team at Arcadia Publishing; Barbara Brinson Curiel; Mary Davis of the Pikes Peak Library District; Gertrude Dial; Ray Drake; Michael Duffy and Rick Leonard; Norma Engleberg; Leland Feitz; Charles Frizzell and Shawn Frizzell; Senator Dennis Gallagher; Reed Grainger; Mike Grant; Dickie Grater; La Jean Greeson; June and Margaret Hack; Buck and Glory Hakes; Lodi, Harold and Ike Hern; Stephanie and J.D. Hilliard; Teresa Huber; Ed Hunter; Richard Wayne Johnson; Joe and Deb; Sally McCready Johnson; Ray Javernick; Jim Keeler; Carol Kenney; The Fabulous Lays Brothers; Mac McCormick; Richard Marold; T.O. Locker; David Martinek; Bonnie and Steve Mackin; Jane Mannon; Brian Marshal; David "Bean"

McCormick; Mel McFarland; Nolan Mick; Mike Moore; Dr. Thomas J. Noel; Cathleen Norman; Mylia Orr; Georganna and Bud Peiffer; Kat Pedersen; Forrest Porter; Mark Rathgeber; Thelma Rathke; Noelle Rathmell; Cookie Ringo; Jackie Roundy; Mary and Bud Sanders; Lori Sewald and Mark Gregory; Ed Sherman; Jack and Betsy Shoup; Tricia Smith; the Snare family; Troy Speakman; Terri Stierhoff; Kathryn Sturdevant; Erik Swanson; Deb Temmer; Randall and Stephanie Terry; Loretta and Art Tremayne; Jeff, Missie and Stubby Trenary; Betty and David Tritz; Thayer Tutt; Professor Stephen Veatch; the Vetter family; Guy and Bryce Vinyard; Paula Waddington; Brian Tim Wellesley; Lisa and Brian Wheatcraft; Linda Wiedman; Maurice Woods; Ohrt Yeager; Marion Zachary, Ruth and Jon Zalewski; all the people who fed me little tidbits of history as they came and went; and of course my dear husband, Corey, whose patience with me knows no boundaries.

INTRODUCTION

During the 1800s, gold booms were nothing new to the United States. From the first official gold rush in North Carolina in 1799 to the Fairbanks gold rush in Alaska beginning in 1902, North America was rife with discoveries of resplendent yellow gold deposits from coast to coast. The California gold rush of 1848 was the first to bring prospectors west in droves. Subsequent discoveries in Arizona, the Dakotas, Idaho, Montana, New Mexico, Oregon and other places would spur further quests for valuable gold metals. The legendary Pikes Peak gold rush of 1858 near Denver would prove that Colorado was a viable producer of glorious gold nuggets. And it was the rush to the Cripple Creek District in 1891 that produced twenty-one million ounces of gold from upward of five hundred mines in just a twenty-four-square-mile area.

Mines sprawling across the hillsides around towns of the district were not uncommon. *Courtesy Cripple Creek District Museum #20068.*

Cripple Creek was initially called Fremont when it was photographed in 1892. *Courtesy Cripple Creek District Museum A 82 23.*

Boomtowns were amazing places. History shows that these areas experienced much mayhem from the time they made mineral discoveries until mining efforts waned and folks moved off to greener pastures. At the beginning of any mining boom, when miners were settling on raw land and in dire need of supplies, lots of people who could provide these items inevitably made an appearance too—so did a host of con artists, wayward women, thieves and other unscrupulous folks who coolly took advantage of the gold and cash filling men's pockets. Their antics added much flavor to American history.

Over three decades, the Cripple Creek District made history as a household phrase across America and even the world. From 1891 to 1916, the district produced $340 million in gold—twice as much as the California gold rush of 1849. But it was hard work. Access to the district was initially made via raw, rough trails and primitive roads. Most made the trek via Ute Pass, an ancient Native trail winding its way up a narrow canyon from Colorado Springs to the east, or from a primitive wagon road leading from the boomtown of Leadville to the west. Here, at nearly ten thousand feet in altitude, early pioneers withstood all kinds of weather to survive. It was not uncommon to see vicious lightning and hailstorms during the summer months, and winters sometimes brought below-zero temperatures and several feet of snow. Only the hardy would survive in such elements as they struggled to settle towns and camps while thousands of men toiled in dangerous underground mines.

The early days of the district, famous as the last big gold boom in Colorado, were quite raucous. Saloons, gambling joints and makeshift brothels popped up in tents and primitive buildings as dozens of cities, towns, communities and camps sprang up. Looking at today's district, encompassing a series of mountains in high terrain, it is hard to imagine the building process. But build the pioneers did, with some of them achieving remarkable engineering feats to construct buildings and mineshafts on the dizzying hillsides and in steep gullies and dipping valleys.

Within the towns of the district, heroes and villains, saints and sinners comingled as schools, churches, businesses, stage stops and railroads slowly but surely made life easier in the thin air. Everyone was scrambling for gold, food, and the bare essentials necessary to stay alive. It is not hard to suppose that these early

CITIES AND TOWNS OF THE CRIPPLE CREEK DISTRICT, 1891 TO 1900

Alta Vista
Altman
Anaconda
Arequa
Barry
Beaver Park
Cameron
Cripple Creek
Eclipse
Elkton
Fremont
Gillette
Goldfield
Independence
Lawrence
Midway
Mound City
Spring Creek
Strattonville/Winfield
Victor

settlers were indeed a scrappy and hardy bunch. Sometimes, the only way to settle a difference of opinion was by exchanging deadly bullets. Other times, men (and also women) merely beat the daylights out of each other, the winner emerging as the one who was "right."

It is not surprising that bar fights, shootouts and murders were quite commonplace in the district, and it didn't help that the El Paso County sheriff in Colorado Springs was over a day's ride away when the district was first formed. Dozens of badmen and bad women made the district memorable as the local mines generated enough gold for some of its millionaires to build a trolley system and several notable buildings and mansions—including the opulent Broadmoor Hotel—in Colorado Springs. Even the dome of the state capitol in Denver has been adorned

The city of Victor grew to be the second largest in the Cripple Creek District. *Courtesy Victor Lowell Thomas Museum.*

with gold from the district, once in 1908 and again during a restoration in 2006.

With the dawn of 1900, the district peaked. Hardrock mining was becoming more difficult and expensive, and some even believed there was little more gold to be found. Gambling and prostitution were eventually outlawed for good. That did not keep gamblers and soiled doves from continuing business on the down-low, but within five years, even they began moving away under their own steam along with thousands of other people. Whole towns were slowly abandoned as only a few diehard families, some of them ranchers before the gold boom began, remained. By 1912, the Cripple Creek District directory told the tale: it was about as thin as a peanut butter sandwich with no peanut butter, and would continue shrinking.

For the next eight decades, the district somehow managed to survive. Although most towns were just shells of their former selves, Cripple Creek and Victor remained afloat in the way of numerous tourist attractions, shops, restaurants, bars and hotels that experienced good cash flow during the summer months. Then in 1989, the Little Ike Tunnel on State Highway 67 suffered a small cave-in, requiring big repairs. Built during the 1890s as

Cripple Creek's Fountain Saloon was just one of many watering holes generously sprinkled throughout the district. *Courtesy Cripple Creek District* Museum A82-262.

part of the Midland Terminal Railroad coming into the district, the tunnel became a one-way thoroughfare after the railroad ceased service in 1949. Because Highway 67 was the only paved road leading into the district at the time, the cities of Cripple Creek and Victor quickly appealed to the state to repair the tunnel. But the state believed Teller County, which maintained the highway, should be responsible for fixing the problem. In turn, Teller County handed the task back to Cripple Creek and Victor, since they were the end destination of the highway before it turned to a dirt road outside of Victor. Visitors, especially those from out of state, were soon laboring under the misconception that there was no other way to access the district. Area businesses began losing money.

In 1990, a group of Cripple Creek businessmen snapped to attention when two similar boomtowns west of Denver, Black Hawk and Central City, began talking about legalizing limited-stakes gambling. The idea caught on in Cripple Creek, but Victor's mayor, James Keeler, refused to even introduce the idea to his council or constituents. And so, on October 1, 1991, limited-stakes gaming became legal in the other three cities. The change in the Cripple Creek District was simply astounding. In the months before opening day, dozens of new casino owners, including those who had owned buildings in Cripple Creek for years, scrambled to upgrade their facilities, acquire casino licenses, learn Colorado's gaming laws and hire the locals and people flooding into town looking for jobs. Real estate prices skyrocketed as buildings were refitted with pseudo-Victorian décor and thousands of slot machines and table games were hauled through their doors. Hundreds of casino workers paid for gaming licenses and scoured Cripple Creek, Victor, the sleepy community of Goldfield and other places to find homes, some of which had not been occupied for decades. Come opening day, seven casinos swung their doors wide open. Many more have opened and closed over time.

In this book are some mighty colorful stories of greed, lust, thievery and murder that were the stuff of a good dime novel back in the day. The district's first and richest millionaire, Winfield Scott Stratton, once uttered, "Too much money is not good for any man. I have too much money and it is not good for me."[1] That was probably true at the time and may still be, even as the district has grown comfortable with its new station in life as a gambling destination. But the amazing stories of how this crazy little piece of Teller County has fared through history remain. Here are a few of them.

1

CRIPPLE CREEK'S
FIRST MURDER VICTIM

The story of the Cripple Creek District begins with Horace Bennett and Julius Myers, a couple of real estate speculators from Denver. The two had been in business for only about a year when, in 1885, they heard about the Pikes Peak Land and Cattle Company high up on the back side of Pikes Peak. The owner, Phillip Ellsworth, had paid $75,000 for the land. There were four homesteads on the property, including two that belonged to ranchers Levi Welty and William Womack. Unfortunately, Ellsworth had not reckoned on the high altitude, close to ten thousand feet, which made farming extremely difficult. When Bennett and Myers offered $25,000 for the Pikes Peak Land and Cattle Company, Ellsworth was only too glad to take it.

Bennett and Myers appear to have been equally naïve about how useless the land they purchased really was. Even so, they optimistically hired Alexander Houseman to oversee things. A second man, George Carr of Kansas, was hired to manage the old Welty homestead, which was renamed the Broken Box Ranch. Bennett and Myers also met Bob Womack, William Womack's son, who was certain there was gold in the area and was searching for it in earnest. Womack had previously mined in other parts of Colorado and knew what he was talking about.

In 1886, Womack staked the Grand View claim and partnered with Edwin Wallace a year later. In 1889, Womack talked his dentist, Dr. John Grannis, into grubstaking him in exchange for a half interest in the mine. When Wallace abandoned his interest, Womack took over and re-staked the claim as the El Paso Mine. Grannis, meantime, hired Professor Henry Lamb of the Colorado College in Colorado Springs to assay Womack's ore. The sample assayed at $250 per ton, spurring the Cripple Creek gold rush.

Quite suddenly, the area was overrun with prospectors, speculators, businessmen and others as makeshift tents popped up everywhere. Streets were graded along the hillsides as Bennett and Myers established the city of Fremont, named for the great explorer John C. Fremont. The post office opened in July 1891 as the town continued to grow. Bennett and Myers were making money hand over fist—so was the Colorado Midland Railroad, which increased its runs from Colorado Springs to three trains a day

Bob Womack's resilience and determination led to the discovery of gold in the district. *Courtesy Cripple Creek District Museum #200121.*

through Divide and Florissant. Both towns had wagon roads leading to the district. Those who could not afford train fare made their way to the district in wagons, on horseback and on foot.

By November, Fremont had thirty platted blocks with lots selling for twenty-five dollars each, or fifty dollars for a corner lot. Their values would rise as the gold boom got underway. A real estate war erupted when some investors from Colorado Springs formed their own town, Hayden Placer, right next to Fremont. Bennett & Myers Company demanded cash for their properties, while Hayden Placer offered payment plans (perhaps thinking the properties would come back to them if the gold boom failed). But Hayden Placer's crucial mistake was outlawing gambling and liquor.

Bennett and Myers coolly took advantage of Hayden Placer's anti-liquor ordinance, declaring that all bettors and tipplers were welcome in Fremont. The combined population soon grew to somewhere between six and eight hundred new citizens. Finally, the postmaster general realized that the name Cripple Creek had already been applied to the creek running through town by a ranch hand, Billy Gibbs, who worked for Levi Welty. In fact, the new gold mining district was being called the "Cripple Creek Gold Mining District." The matter was settled when postal authorities announced that both Hayden Placer and Fremont would share one post office, Cripple

Creek, as of June 1892. To the incoming settlers, it didn't seem to matter what the new town was called so long as the ground continued to produce rich ore. Within a short time, a slew of buildings and tents were going up all over Cripple Creek. They included wholesale liquor houses, gambling joints, dance halls and saloons—lots and lots of saloons. These were the places that would spur some of the most colorful stories about the district's early days.

Ute Pass, shown here in 1885, was a most viable way to bring supplies to the Cripple Creek District. *National Archives & Records.*

For miners arriving in Cripple Creek, especially sans any family, the nights could be especially lonely. A musty tent or dreary cabin was excruciatingly dull compared to the bright lights, gay laughter and music emanating from the downtown area. A little gold dust could buy a meal, beer or whiskey or a lady for the evening. The most boisterous of men in these places would shuffle roughly around one another, trying to show their importance with bragging rights about how well their mining claims were doing. Those who had no gold, however—having lost it on a bet or by partaking in a drink or three—might hang out and look for a chance to recoup their losses, even if it meant stealing. And that is where Charles Hudspeth came in.

Hudspeth had been in Colorado since at least 1880, when he was employed at the ranch of William Smith in Weld County. He was described as "mulatto" or of mixed heritage. Said heritage very well may have led to hardships in a time when America expressed much prejudice against Blacks. By 1882, Hudspeth had already encountered the latest in a long string of bullies in his life. His problems were destined to escalate.

In January, Hudspeth stabled his horses at Craig's Ranch near Castle Rock, north of Colorado Springs, and wandered into the Star Saloon. A man named Alex Collins invited Hudspeth to a drink, which he accepted. The two began discussing an upcoming horse race, on which Hudspeth expressed an interest in placing a bet. But when he explained that he could offer up only his saddle against $30 if his horse won, a drunken Collins scoffed at him. The bet was $500, Collins said. Hudspeth couldn't afford that and said so. Collins, however, claimed the man had made a bona fide bet and began teasing him, throwing fake punches and even pretending to draw a gun on him. One of Collins's friends, Tom Little, recommended that Hudspeth leave the bar.

A frustrated and angry Hudspeth left the Star and went to Little's house, where he found a gun, and returned to the saloon. When Little took the firearm from him, Hudspeth left again and went back to Craig's Ranch. Craig had a revolver too—everybody did, in those days—so Hudspeth took it and returned to the Star once more. The rest of the evening remained quiet, until Hudspeth left to turn in for the night. Outside were Collins, Little and another man, Peter Anderson. Everyone was in their cups. Later, in court, Hudspeth would admit that he remembered calling out, "Alex Collins, you have been threatening my life all day—are you ready to die? I am!"[2] Two shots rang out from Hudspeth's revolver. The second one hit Collins in the stomach. He staggered and fell, begging Hudspeth to stop shooting. A doctor was called to attend the injured man, but he soon died.

Castle Rock, pictured here around 1910, changed very little in the years after Hudspeth was there. *Wikimedia Commons.*

Although witnesses testified that Collins was a dangerous man, Hudspeth was found guilty of manslaughter. As prisoner no. 964, he was sentenced to five years of hard labor at the Colorado State Penitentiary in Cañon City.

Upon his release in 1888, Hudspeth moved to Florence, one town over from Cañon City. In February 1892, the *Rocky Mountain News* noted that he had found work as a stage driver for Al Salmon's new Florence and Cripple Creek Stage. The stage line wound its way along a steep meandering trail formerly used by area Natives that was first called Eight Mile Canyon, then Ute Canyon and finally Phantom Canyon. The trail came out near today's City of Victor. When the road was finished, the *Rocky Mountain News* of April 1 described the stage line's premiere:

> *The Florence and Cripple Creek road is operating successfully. Travel is on the increase and the stages* [are] *making better time than was expected by the management until the roads should dry up. A trip was made today in six hours and four minutes. This time, the management claims, in a week or two can be cut down to four hours. The stages leave promptly every morning*

A historic bridge in Phantom Canyon remains in place even today. *Author's collection.*

at 7 o'clock, and gets in from Fremont at 3 p.m. There has been no snow or rain for about fifteen days, and the recent heavy snow in the cañon is about all gone, and the road is becoming smooth and dry.[3]

On the same day the article broke, Charles Hudspeth drove one of the first coaches of the stage line up to Fremont and decided to spend the night. By evening, he was getting drunk and having a good time at Charlie Christolph's Iron Clad Dance Hall. Inside was a bar and a dance floor, where girls in pretty dresses awaited their customers. A piano player was employed to call out to the men present to pick a girl and pay the bartender for the dance before being admitted to the dance floor.

On this particular night at the Iron Clad, Reuben "Rube" Miller was employed as the dance caller and piano player. Little was known about Miller, except that he originally hailed from Nebraska and had come to Fremont just a few weeks previous. The *Rocky Mountain News* would later note that Miller "was well liked in the camp, being of a quiet disposition and a light spirit."[4] Living with Miller was Nina Smith, a Leadville dance hall girl who had made the trip with her man to the new camp. Nina was most likely present when an issue arose between Charles Hudspeth and the Iron Clad's bartender, John McMichael.

Initial reports claimed that around 3:00 a.m., following an argument between McMichael and Hudspeth, the latter left the dance hall in a "great rage," stole a revolver from a nearby tent, returned to the Iron Clad and fired at McMichael through a window.[5] Hudspeth missed his intended mark. Miller, who was standing next to the bartender, was hit instead. The bullet struck the piano player just above his right temple, passed through the top of his head and split, half of it coming out the other side and the other half remaining lodged in his brain. The *Aspen Daily Chronicle* claimed that afterward, Hudspeth simply "ran down to his room and went to bed."[6] Stumbled was more like it, since newspapers also stated that Hudspeth was intoxicated. Other newspapers decided to make the most of the shooting with blaring, inaccurate headlines like "A Desperate Fremont Negro Shoots a Stage Driver Down in Cold Blood," and expressing the opinion that the "shooting was a cold blooded attempt to murder" as Hudspeth walked "coolly away" from the scene.[7]

There was, of course, more to the story. One version verified that Hudspeth and another Black man named Bob Mayberry were already in the bar when one J.F. Parker, who was White and also drunk, approached McMichael with the complaint that his watch was suddenly missing. Whether Hudspeth was accused of the theft was never made clear, but somehow, he was thrown into the mix as heated words were exchanged between himself, Parker and the bartender. In that account, Hudspeth left the Iron Clad, returned with a gun and attempted to shoot at McMichael, but during this first attempt, someone was able to slap the gunman's arm. The bullet lodged in the ceiling instead. By then McMichael had grabbed a club, and before a second shot could be fired, he struck Hudspeth in the head, leaving an ugly gash. Then he wrestled the assailant to the door and physically threw him out.

As the dancing and drinking resumed, Hudspeth staggered to a nearby tent and borrowed a second gun. One of the girls in the dance hall saw him as he approached a window from the outside and screamed, "Look out!"[8] Just then, Hudspeth fired at McMichael through the window. The first shot hit Miller by mistake. A second shot hit the bar. As Miller fell, McMichael hotfooted it out the back door and headed up the back stairs to his room above the dance hall to retrieve his own revolver. Hudspeth followed him and fired a third shot but missed. Back in the dance hall, Mayberry began firing his own gun in the air, which scared the crowd even more. Hudspeth had indeed staggered back to his own room when Deputy Sheriff Peter Bales found and arrested him. Mayberry and Parker were arrested as well. All three were taken to Fremont's tiny jail.

By now, an ugly mob had formed with the intent to administer their own version of frontier justice. Luckily, Bales heard about the lynch mob and quickly hustled his prisoners into a buckboard. The only way to keep the other inmates at the jail safe was to set them free. They "were given their liberty and told to take to the mountains and they were not slow to obey," according to the *Rocky Mountain News*.[9] With his prisoners secured, Bales took off for Florissant at breakneck speed, thereby saving Hudspeth, Mayberry and Parker from "a neck-tie party," reported Pueblo's *Daily Chieftain*.[10] As the wagon hastened toward Florissant, Sheriff M.F. Bowers in Colorado Springs was notified and hurried to meet Bales and receive the prisoners. The *Rocky Mountain News* praised Bales, "who unflinchingly did his duty" and made sure justice was served.[11] The charge against Hudspeth was officially changed to murder when Reuben Miller died at ten o'clock that morning.

As Hudspeth's trial got underway in Colorado Springs, a second victim of his actions made the newspapers: Nina Smith. The girl was absolutely devastated at the loss of her man. The *Rocky Mountain News* reported on April 25 that Nina had been "despondent and drinking" since the shooting and kept threatening to kill herself.[12] *Svensk-Amerikanska Western*, a Swedish newspaper, intimated that Nina "had been suffering from melancholy for some time and, moreover, had devoted herself too much to [Bacchus's] service and worship. She sobbed incessantly."[13] On April 24, Nina downed a fatal dose of morphine. She was likely buried in what would become Cripple Creek's Mt. Pisgah Cemetery.[14]

The deaths of Reuben Miller and Nina Smith were not soon forgotten. A few months later, Charlie Christolph made the papers again. His dance hall was known as the Great View when one Paddy Burns got drunk and engaged in a fight with several others. It was Christolph himself who suddenly began shooting into the crowd. In this instance, someone was

Charles Hudspeth's mugshot at the State Pen was his second one in a decade. *Colorado State Archives.*

able to hit the gun as it fired, "and the bullet was imbedded in the ceiling, instead of a human being," said the *Rocky Mountain News.* The paper also called the dance hall "the toughest in the camp."[15] Authorities agreed, and a Constable Nolan closed the Great View down as he swore out a warrant for Christolph. As for Charles Hudspeth, he became a guest of the state for a second time. As prisoner no. 2959, he was once again incarcerated at the Colorado State Penitentiary. The last documentation of him lies with the 1900 census, which finds him still incarcerated there. What became of him after that is anyone's guess.

THE HEIST AT THE HOTEL VICTOR

istorians are well familiar with the Woods family, who moved to the booming Cripple Creek District in 1892. Warren Woods and his sons, Harry and Frank, had already honed their business smarts in Illinois and Ohio before heading west with lots of money in their pockets. Upon their arrival, they formed the Woods Investment Company, purchased a 136-acre claim in 1893 for $1,000 and laid out the new city of Victor a few miles from Cripple Creek. The second-largest city in the district was named for a nearby homesteader, Victor C. Adams, who had been in the area since 1888. Because Victor was laid out on a placer claim, the Woods Investment Company could honestly advertise that every lot sold would likely yield some gold (some buyers may have been unaware, however, that they received only surface rights). The Woodses then began building several fabulous structures for what they hoped would become the wealthiest town in the district. In order to attract wealthy investors, a first-class hotel was needed.

Construction on the Hotel Victor began in March 1894. But no sooner was Frank Woods overseeing the digging of the foundation than a twenty-inch vein of rich ore was unearthed. The newly discovered Gold Coin Mine was staked as the Hotel Victor was moved over a bit to accommodate the mine. A few months later, J.E. Rizer of the Monday Evening Club in Pueblo would be among the first to sample the amenities at the completed project in September. "This elegant new hotel has just been opened, and we will never forget our kind treatment there," Rizer told the *Cripple Creek Morning*

Journal. "The hotel is completely equipped with all modern conveniencies [*sic*] and deserves and will receive most generous patronage. Our rapacious appetites were more than satisfied by the sumptuous meal which Victor's generosity provided for us, and we delayed the departure of the train an hour in order to partake fully of their hospitality."[16]

The Hotel Victor quickly became the social center of the city. The next time the *Morning Journal* mentioned it was in October, when the hotel announced a grand Fireman's Ball on the tenth. "This will be the grandest ball ever given in the Cripple Creek district," the newspaper promised. "The boys extend a cordial invitation to our sister cities and assure one and all a pleasant time. Tickets, $1." A special train was secured to bring partygoers from all over the district. Notably, the article made sure to point out that "no objectionable characters will be admitted."[17] Little did anyone know that some mighty "objectional characters" would indeed soon tarnish the hotel's fine reputation.

Just after midnight on Friday, October 12, three masked men walked into the hotel's gambling parlors. The games were run by Sam Yarnell,

The Hotel Victor was by far the fanciest in town. *Courtesy Victor Lowell Thomas Museum.*

a well-respected citizen who dabbled in politics and supported the local miners' unions. But Yarnell was not there that night; only a faro game and one roulette wheel were in play as four to six men placed their bets. It was the perfect time to rob the place. Faro dealer James Lacey looked up to see the robbers coming into the room, their revolvers drawn. Everyone was ordered to put their hands up as one of the bandits grabbed the bank roll, containing between $400 and $700, from the table. The threesome then backed out of the room and disappeared into the night. Police were summoned as someone found a lone saddled horse wandering the streets. The animal was recognized as belonging to William Welty's livery stable in Cripple Creek.

The horse was quickly ridden to Welty's, where it was ascertained that three men had indeed procured three horses earlier in the evening. Welty gave only a vague description of the group: one was around 160 pounds with a red face and a heavy moustache. A second, smaller man had a dark complexion. The third accomplice was tall with fair skin. A few hours later, a man named Shaw rode into Cripple Creek from Bull Hill. He was leading Welty's other two horses. Shaw said that two men had given the horses to him and paid him to return them to the stables.

Deputy Sheriff K.C. Sterling rounded up an armed posse and rode off in the direction of Bull Hill. "This is the boldest holdup that has occurred in the state for a long time," commented the *Morning Journal*, adding to the general opinion that the thieves would soon be caught.[18] Two days later, police got word that the robbers were planning to attend the Sunday races at Charles Tutt and Spencer Penrose's horse track at the district town of Gillett. Shortly after the Midland Terminal Railroad had reached Gillett back in July, the budding bachelor millionaires built the track and a casino in the field just northeast of the town. Known locally as "Sportsman's Park," the track was one of the few outdoor venues where men could carouse and bet their money on horses. Sheriff Sterling and his men planned to be there when the robbers came to the park.

Sure enough, the sheriff's party almost immediately singled out Jimmy Cannon and Tommy Short, who were identified as participating in the robbery. They were with a large group of friends, who immediately began arguing with the lawmen. A few threats were hurled in the officers' direction before Sterling and his men handcuffed Cannon and Short, deposited them into a wagon and left for the jail in Cripple Creek. It would not, however, be the end of the matter. The accused were employed as miners in the district, and it was only recently that a local labor war had been settled.

Gillett was the first city to be reached by the Midland Terminal Railroad. *Courtesy Cripple Creek District Museum.*

This first labor strike had started back in January, when several mining companies decided to extend the workday from eight hours to nine at the same rate of pay of three dollars per day. On February 1, nearly five hundred disgruntled miners walked off the job. Soon, neighbors were pitched against neighbors and friends against friends as everyone took sides during the strike. For four long months, mine owners and union miners battled it out until a compromise was reached in June. Work resumed, but hard feelings continued to linger for much longer. The arrests of Jimmy Cannon and Tommy Short simply brought those hard feelings right back to the surface.

Because the district was still part of El Paso County at the time, the only court was in Colorado Springs. Sterling planned to take his prisoners there the following day—until that evening, when he got word that a large angry group of miners was meeting at the town of Altman above Victor. Also present was C.B. Flynn, who owned the Nightingale Mine. "Tom Short and Jim Cannon have been working for me for the past three months," he told a reporter. "I attended the benefit ball at Altman last Friday and know that both men were present. They are hard-working, sober miners, and I know, as well as all who know them, that they are not criminals."[19]

Many others soon voiced their agreement with Flynn's statement that Cannon and Short had indeed been at the Altman benefit for a fellow miner, Dan Morrison. Before long, the law was judged as seeking vengeance against two innocent miners because of the strike. A group numbering as many as one hundred men was now making its way to Cripple Creek for a word with Deputy Sterling.

Of course, Sterling wanted nothing to do with the mob that was about to descend on him. Along with deputies E.B. Eyer and Lew Hayes, the officer quickly ushered the prisoners into a wagon and headed to Florissant eighteen miles away. Sterling hoped to board a Colorado Midland train bound for Colorado Springs. But it was so late that only one more train was scheduled to come through Divide, eight miles from Florissant. Sterling's group quickly rode there in hopes of catching the train.

All might have gone smoothly had Sterling and his officers not made a crucial mistake. The wagon had pulled into a livery barn by the railroad tracks. The prisoners, manacled together at the wrists, were taken out and made to stand near the rear of the wagon as Eyer and Hayes unhitched the team. Tommy Short would later relay what happened next: "We were arrested, but did not want to come down here [to Colorado Springs]," he said. "We wanted to be tried at Victor. If we came down here, Cannon said, we would stay in jail three or four months. Cannon made the suggestion that we would try to get away."[20]

The prisoners had noticed that the officers' Winchesters lay right in the back of the wagon, within their reach. When Sterling and one of his men started off to look for some blankets, Cannon and Short managed to grab one of the rifles from the wagon. As they wrestled together to get a purchase on the gunstock, Sterling ran up and tried to intervene. He was struck by one or both men, one of whom pulled the pistol from the officer's belt as he fell. The gun went off and hit the roof of the barn as the escapees began running, still manacled together, down the railroad track.

Tommy Short later testified that he and Cannon dove behind a stack of railroad ties as Sterling chased them, commanding them to stop and firing at them. One shot hit Short in the leg. "We give up!" he shouted. At the same moment, Cannon returned the gunfire, and Sterling fired again. Cannon was struck in the face and the chest, dying within seconds. When asked if he felt the officers were at fault for Cannon's death, Short told the court, "It looks that way, after a man said 'We surrender.'"[21]

As to whether Short and Cannon really were guilty of the Hotel Victor robbery, Deputy Sterling verified to the *Morning Journal* that James Lacey had positively identified the men as two of the robbers. Stories about the way the whole incident played out were left to the newspapers, whose grandiose verbiage and prejudice pretty much muddled up the truth. One interesting

Men line up at the depot at Divide, very near the spot where Deputy Sterling shot it out with Jimmy Cannon and Tommy Short. *Courtesy Denver Public Library X-7727.*

note was that a union miner's card was found in Jimmy Cannon's pockets. Although his membership had been in arrears for several months, he had happened to dutifully pay his dues in full the day after the robbery. The court finally ruled that both prisoners had been resisting arrest when they were shot. Word of the third alleged robber at the Hotel Victor, meanwhile, was never even mentioned.

The shooting of two miners, one of whom died, did not ease tensions in the district. C.B. Flynn not only put up Tommy Short's bail and had him installed at the St. Nicholas Hospital in Cripple Creek to recuperate, but he also paid for Jimmy Cannon's burial in Cripple Creek. How much time Short served was not reported, but the killing of Cannon and Flynn's kindness toward Short was, as far as many were concerned, the end of trying to solve the robbery of the Hotel Victor. Most interesting is that as of April 1897 there was a new constable in Victor. By coincidence or design, his name was Tom Short.

There is also an interesting side note about Mr. Flynn: in 1895, the enigmatic mining man married Pearl DeVere, who was in the process of becoming Cripple Creek's most famous madam. A native of Indiana, the divine Ms. DeVere had traveled extensively to New York, Chicago and other places before coming to Colorado. The lady was destined to be a courtesan, the upper echelon of working girls everywhere, and even spent time with a famous gambler of the time, Billy Deutsch, who died in 1893. She was hopping between her flowering parlor house in Cripple Creek and Denver when she apparently met Flynn.

Notable is that days after the marriage, C.B. Flynn appeared on the guest list at the opulent Brown Palace Hotel in Denver. Was the new Mrs. Flynn with him? It is hard to say, as Flynn soon traveled to Mexico, where some of his mining interests lay. There he remained, only occasionally visiting the Cripple Creek District to check on his other mining interests while Pearl built her brothel, the Old Homestead, into the fanciest parlor house the district would ever see. Tragically, the lady died in 1897 of an accidental morphine overdose following one of her famous Saturday night soirees. Flynn did not attend her funeral, but Pearl's estate record revealed she had lent the man over $1,000 during their marriage. Flynn settled the debt in the amount of $199.50 and disappeared into history.

THE KILLING OF
RICHARD NEWELL

For Richard Newell Jr., the chance to be a part of the booming Cripple Creek District was one of a lifetime. In 1891, he married his true love, Elizabeth "Lizzie" Harris, in Ohio, who gave birth to two children before the family relocated to Colorado. Shortly after their arrival in 1893, Newell was hired as superintendent of construction for the Midland Terminal Railroad (MTRR). The new line was a spur of the Colorado Midland Railroad coming out of Colorado Springs via Ute Pass and was slowly but surely being built from Divide to the District. Life looked promising indeed.

The new rail line was not without its problems. Having switched midway from narrow gauge to standard gauge rails before it even made it to a halfway point at the community of Midland, there were soon rumors that the railroad was in trouble. Pueblo's *Colorado Daily Chieftain* told how Newell had "stated emphatically that work had not stopped. The grading has nearly all been completed where it can be completed now, and the rails are now being laid."[22] Within two weeks, Newell promised, the tracks to Midland would be finished so train passengers could make it that far before catching a stage into the district.

In March 1894, a new problem developed for the MTRR. The law allowed railroads to obtain rights-of-way to cross over private property. The idea did not appeal to property owners, since it would prevent them from using their own land. Only if the right-of-way was abandoned would the land revert to the original owners. The railroads could also hire special officers to enforce the right-of-way and to arrest anyone caught trespassing—including the landowners themselves. There was another issue as well: in the great rush to finish the railroad, Newell soon realized that it would be impossible to build a direct route to Cripple Creek from the next stop, Gillett, due to a 750-foot drop along the last two miles coming into town. Instead, the tracks would have to continue to the budding camp of Grassy (later renamed Cameron) and on to the city of Victor. It would take longer and cost more, but Newell and his team had no other choice. The railroad reached Grassy in the autumn of 1894, and construction crews continued laying tracks toward Winfield Scott Stratton's Independence Mine and Victor.

Further complicating matters was that the MTRR was in a heated contest with the Florence & Cripple Creek Railroad (F&CC), which was building its own line up Phantom Canyon to Victor. The pressure was great for the MTRR to reach the district before the F&CC did. Added to the strain was that Lizzie Newell died suddenly at the couple's Colorado Springs home on November 26. Newell had to drop everything to take his wife's body back to Ohio for burial and return as quickly as possible to the work at hand.

Lizzie had not been in her grave for a month when her husband was tasked with evicting some difficult occupants of a cabin standing in the way of the MTRR tracks near the Independence Mine. Sylvester Yeoman,

Photographer William Henry Jackson captured a wagon train headed to the Cripple Creek District, the only way to get there before the railroads were built. *Courtesy Denver Public Library WHJ-826.*

Midland has changed very little since the days when a small depot served the Midland Terminal Railroad. *Author's collection.*

a partner in the Black Wonder Mine, had just recently won a lawsuit suit for damages after the MTRR tracks blazed through his mining claim without so much as a howd'ya do. But Yeoman's cabin still stood on the right-of-way, blocking construction. On the afternoon of December 19, Newell hopped on the MTRR at Gillett and headed toward Yeoman's cabin. What happened next was later revealed in court testimonies from the newspapers.

According to a man named Hoskins, he was preparing dinner at the cabin when the train pulled up. Newell, said Hoskins, "jumped from the car and walked rapidly toward the cabin, entering the open door." Also in the cabin at the time was Aaron Van Houten. "Where is the man I saw the other day?" Newell demanded. "I guess it is me you mean, Mr. Newell," Van Houten answered. "No," Newell said, "it is not you I mean at all. I mean the man I saw the other day." Hoskins piped up. "I guess it is Mr. Yeoman you mean, Mr. Newell."[23] Newell remained confused as he handed a letter to Van Houten, thinking he was Yeoman. The letter merely confirmed that the railroad would pay $150 for the damages regarding the Black Wonder claim and would be paying no more.

As Van Houten read the letter, Hoskins looked outside and saw conductor Ira Blizzard and another man on the train. Van Houten finished reading the letter and began, "Well, Mr. Newell, that is all right, but—" before Newell cut him off. "I shall pull this cabin down tomorrow morning!" he declared.

"I don't know about that," Van Houten warned, but Newell was resolute. "I will pull it down anyhow," he threatened again, and stepped outside. The men began arguing, each of them talking at once. When Hoskins looked up again, he saw Van Houten with "his fist up against Newell and Newell had his hands raised." Hoskins quickly began setting the pots of food on the floor to keep them from burning so he could watch the fisticuffs. "You come outside and fight," Newell dared Van Houten.[24]

"You son-of-a-bitch!" Van Houten retorted as he pulled a rifle from his bunk bed. Hoskins was still scrambling to get the pots off the stove when he heard Newell say, "That is the only way you will come out," and the sound of a shot filled the air. The two men on the train jumped down and ran toward the cabin as Hoskins watched Newell, who began staggering sideways and holding his side. Blizzard and the other man reached Newell just as he fell into their arms. They began carrying him to the train as the conductor disembarked to help. "I don't allow any [expletive] to pull a cabin down after me," Van Houten shouted at him. "You don't need to talk about it, my friend," the conductor responded calmly, "that man is dead."[25]

Victor deputy sheriff Len Jackson was notified and rode to the Black Wonder cabin with six other men. Newspapers said that Van Houten went for his pistol but gave up when four Winchesters were pointed in his direction. Later that day, Van Houten and the body of Richard Newell made the trip together on the evening train to Colorado Springs under heavy guard. Van Houten was taken to jail as Newell's body was prepared for shipment to Ohio. In court, Van Houten testified that Newell appeared to be either intoxicated or very angry when he came to the cabin. Newell's exact words, he said, were, "I am going to tear this cabin down if I have to kill you people to do it." Not only that, but Newell allegedly heaped a mess of abusive language on Van Houten, tried to hit him and threatened to "come in there and take the gun away from you and kill you."[26] Van Houten also claimed that he only shot Newell when the man began drawing his own pistol. Other witnesses verified that none of Van Houten's testimony was true. In the end, the man was charged with first-degree murder. His trial was set for December 1895.

Sylvester Yeoman, meanwhile, remained a free man. The Black Wonder cabin was finally torn down so the MTRR could resume construction, and the railroad rolled into Victor in late December. The following month, the *Colorado Springs Weekly Gazette* published a most interesting article stating that several witnesses—including three attorneys, reporters from the *Denver Times*

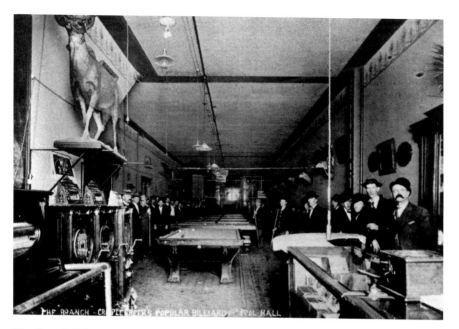

The Branch Saloon, where Sylvester Yeoman spilled his guts to a newspaper reporter. *Courtesy Cripple Creek District Museum.*

and Cripple Creek and even Yeoman's landlord—testified that previous to the shooting they heard Yeoman talking of "what he would do to the officials" of the railroad if they dared come onto his claim and that he had a man stationed at the cabin just in case.[27] The most damning evidence came from M.J. Collins, a Cripple Creek reporter who accompanied Yeoman to the second floor of the Branch Saloon on Bennett Avenue the night of Newell's murder. Yeoman produced a letter, hidden in his shoe, that he had written to Van Houten with instructions to stay in the cabin and refuse to vacate it until directed otherwise.

Van Houten's trial lasted but two days, and he was found guilty. Grand Junction's *Daily Sentinel* commented that the verdict seemed to surprise Van Houten to a great degree, as he had been under the impression that he was doing right by Yeoman. "It's about what I expected," the *Walsenburg World* later quoted Van Houten as saying. "I'm from Bull Hill, and no Bull Hill man can get justice at Colorado Springs."[28] But the killer must have been mighty thankful when the decision to hang him was overturned. Instead, Governor Albert Wills McIntire commuted his sentence to life in prison at the Colorado State Penitentiary in Cañon City.

When the city of Gillett was officially platted in 1897, one of the streets was named Newell after the fallen railroad man. Van Houten, meanwhile, made a model prisoner. In 1901, he appealed to the Board of Pardons. His lawyer pointed out that not only did Van Houten have permission to occupy Sylvester Yeoman's cabin, but the MTRR had never officially paid Yeoman for the damages owed to him as well. Under protest by those who remembered the case, acting governor D.C. Coates officially pardoned Aaron Van Houten in July 1902 and remained publicly unapologetic about his decision. Van Houten was never heard from in Colorado again.

4

THE ROBBERY OF THE FLORENCE AND CRIPPLE CREEK TRAIN

*S*herman Crumley. Kid Wallace. The Smoke-Eyed Kid. The names of these characters would fit nicely in a dime novel from the Old West. But while their exploits never became the stuff of Wild West adventure books, their time and crime in the Cripple Creek District were very real. These were the outlaws, along with a handful of others, who were involved with the first and only robbery of the Florence and Cripple Creek Railroad (F&CC) in 1895.

The F&CC's illustrious beginnings date to 1891, when Florence merchant James A. McCandless surveyed Phantom Canyon. Despite the steep and curvy trail, McCandless and others believed it was possible to eventually build a railroad, which they did beginning in December 1893. On June 30, 1894, the F&CC steamed through the city of Victor to Cripple Creek as citizens cheered the coming of the rails. On the return trip on July 2, unfortunately, the baggage car and both coaches of the F&CC derailed at the small town of Anaconda. One man died and twenty-one others were injured.

By March 1895, the F&CC had recovered quite nicely, despite needing "helper engines" from the whistle stop of Alta Vista to assist the daily trains coming into Victor. Then came the night of March 23. Earlier that evening, a well-known faro dealer named Grant Crumley was working at Cripple Creek's Branch Saloon when he noticed a group of businessmen from St. Louis throwing lots of cash around. Those same men were planning to board the F&CC to Florence later that night. Crumley happened to mention this

The wreck of the Florence and Cripple Creek train at Anaconda, July 1894. *Courtesy Cripple Creek District Museum.*

to his brother, Sherman, who is said to have been the brains behind what happened next.

Around 9:30 that evening, Passenger Train No. 6 had just left Victor. As the train pulled out, an unseen man hopped aboard one of the "blind" baggage cars, an early term for a train car with only a door on one end of the car instead of doors on each end. The train had just crossed a trestle over the south fork of Wilson Creek near the town of Lawrence when the mysterious man climbed into the engine compartment. Pointing a revolver at Engineer Pope and the man tending the firebox, the gunman commanded the men to stop the train. As the train ground to a halt, more men came aboard.

One robber made his way through the train's sleeper car, taking money, rings and watches from passengers in the amount of somewhere between $800 and $1,000. Meanwhile, four to five other robbers broke into the mail car. The group rifled through the freight tags on various boxes and bags but opened nothing. The express messenger in the car was next forced to lead the men to the coach cars, where it was guessed that "two or three gold watches and some money" were taken from passengers.[29] The robbers were dressed in miners' garb, with slouch hats on their heads and masks over their faces. They also appeared quite jovial as they worked.

The robbery took about half an hour in its entirety. The bandits disembarked, but when Engineer Pope began backing the train toward

Victor, he was stopped and forcibly directed to keep heading down Phantom Canyon. The thieves escaped on foot. Lawmen from the district and Florence were notified of the robbery and took off after the robbers as the F&CC offered a $500 reward for their capture. It did not take long before bloodhounds led Cripple Creek constable Lou Lambert to some outbuildings near the Strong Mine at the edge of Victor. Five men—Sherman Crumley, James (aka William) Gibson, Bob "The Smoke-Eyed Kid" Taylor, Louis Vanneck (also occasionally spelled Vannick) and Frank "Kid" Wallace— were rounded up.[30]

Some of the alleged robbers already had records or were at least known for their shenanigans around the district. Taylor, born Robert Earnest Lewis, had already served time at the Kansas State Penitentiary for robbery at the age of sixteen in 1881, once ran with outlaw Henry Starr's gang and escaped from an Oklahoma jail in 1893. He, along with Sherman Crumley, had allegedly participated in the tar and feathering of Adjutant General Thomas J. Tarsney at Colorado Springs just the year before.[31] In addition, Taylor was a former employee of the Strong Mine. Most surprisingly, he had recently been working as a deputy sheriff in Pueblo, where he killed bartender Jack Leach. The court ruled the shooting as self-defense.

On March 26, the five suspected train robbers were taken by Sheriff Bowers to the jail in Colorado Springs. Wallace and Crumley were almost

The tiny town of Lawrence was the closest community to the robbery of the Florence and Cripple Creek train. *Courtesy Cripple Creek District Museum.*

immediately released due to lack of evidence. Taylor claimed he had spent the evening of the robbery in Victor with another man, Jack Smith, before returning to his cabin at the Strong Mine with James Gibson, playing cards late into the evening and going to bed. But Smith was already known to the authorities as a troublemaker who enjoyed shooting up the district town of Altman when he was drunk; in fact, Smith would die in a shoot-out with Marshal Jack Kelley the following May.

The authorities didn't buy Taylor's story. In April, he and Gibson appeared at a preliminary hearing. Bond was set at $10,000 for each man. Within a month, as more details about the robbery came forth, deputies were ordered to round up the men who had been released. Wallace was actually walking alongside a deputy sheriff in Victor when Marshal Sherman Bell informed him that he was under arrest again. Wallace tried to pull his gun, but Constable Lupton attacked the boy from behind and got the weapon away from him. Crumley was also apprehended. That same day, a man named O.C. "Sam" Wilder also was arrested in connection with the train robbery.

For the next several months, newspapers diligently reported on the robbers as their trials commenced. Vanneck testified that Gibson knew nothing about the train robbery, but that he, Crumley, Taylor, Wallace and Wilder were the real perpetrators. It was Taylor's idea, he said, to rob the F&CC. Several reliable witnesses, including the superintendent and employees of the Strong Mine, testified that Taylor and Gibson were playing cards in a cabin all night, just as the prisoners said. Wilder, a watchman at the mine, was working on the night of the robbery and had just been paid, besides. Very little evidence was produced placing Crumley at the scene of the crime. But Wallace, according to Vanneck, had definitely been a willing participant in the robbery.

Around this time, newspapers began taking an interest in Kid Wallace. He came from Nebraska and was only seventeen years old. In court, said the *Rocky Mountain News*, Wallace "looked white and sick. His head dropped back on the top of his chair as if he could not hold it up, and his eyes were closed a good part of the time." It was further noted that Wallace had just come to the district from Missouri some ten days before the robbery. When was asked which town he was from in Nebraska, the boy turned to the judge and told him softly, "I decline to answer simply for the reason that I don't want my people to know where I am."[32]

In the end, the jury could not reach a verdict. The prisoners were temporarily set free as the *Colorado Daily Chieftain* in Pueblo took up the call for pity on Kid Wallace. The paper called him "alone, a forlorn homeless, neglected boy…who only needed a mother's love and care to grow up into a useful citizen."[33] Other newspapers chimed in. "Something ought to be done for 'Kid Wallace,'" lectured the *Rocky Mountain News*. "He is only a boy with a boy's ideas of life warped by reading dime novels and associating with toughs. He is worth saving and by no means past the point where reformation is possible." A second article told of how the Kid's tears had trickled down his "thin cheeks" and "dropped on his limp and ragged collar" before a mistrial was declared.[34]

Despite the sympathy expressed for Wallace, he was included when an all-new trial of the train robbers began in September. This time, only Wallace, Taylor and Wilder were accused. The new trial included a slew of new witnesses, from F&CC employees and passengers to detective J.W. Hawkins, who knew of Taylor's rowdy past. From what the papers said, Hawkins knew Taylor's wife, Nell, even better and had even written some love letters to her. The judge threw this evidence out. In the end, all three men were convicted of robbing the F&CC train.

The prisoners were led from the El Paso County Courthouse in chains. Taylor, who had laughed when the verdict was announced and was now chained to Wilder, suddenly lunged at Hawkins, who was in front of him. Witnesses believed Taylor was going for Hawkins's gun, but he was only able to give Hawkins a swift kick in the leg, making him stumble on the steps. Hawkins remarked that it was a good thing Taylor was in chains and perhaps even smiled a bit; during the new trial, it had been discovered that Taylor was also wanted for train robbery in Oklahoma and other crimes in Washington. Taylor and Wilder were each given ten years in the state penitentiary at Cañon City, while Wallace received eight years. The latter requested to be sent to reform school instead but was denied. Wilder would serve only a small portion of his sentence; by 1900, he was back in the Cripple Creek District, working as a timberman on the Elkhorn Mine. But if the F&CC robbery had faded from people's minds, a most violent event in January of that year would remind them.

On January 22, 1900, four convicts managed to escape the Colorado State Penitentiary. Among them was Kid Wallace. The other three were Thomas Reynolds, C.E. Wagner and Anton Woode. The latter prisoner was especially notable since, at the age of eleven in 1893, he had become the youngest convict at the pen after killing a man in Denver. All four prisoners were working together in the boiler room when Wagner hatched a plan to escape when a guard came to escort the men to dinner. Wagner

The *Rocky Mountain News* published pictures on January 24 of Woode, Wallace, Wagner and Reynolds as lawmen looked for the outlaws. *Public domain.*

reasoned they could overtake the guard and escape over the high wall surrounding the prison. Since young Woode was a pet of sorts among the guards, it was decided not to tell the boy about the plan until it was being carried out.

At ten o'clock that evening, night watch captain William Rooney came to escort the prisoners to dinner and was duly attacked. A panicked Kid Wallace stabbed Rooney repeatedly with a homemade knife and, by accident or design, pierced the man's heart. The prisoners were scurrying across the yard to the prison wall, with Woode in tow, when they encountered another night captain and a prison guard. The officers were subdued, bound and gagged as somebody returned to the boiler room and shut off the lights to the entire grounds. Using previously made pipes with hooks on one end, the escapees were able to scale the wall. Two guards witnessed the escape, and one of them even fired a shot, but the prisoners were out of sight by the time the alarm sounded. Reynolds and Wagner headed toward Florence. Wallace and Woode, meanwhile, made the unwise decision to head toward the Cripple Creek District. A slew of angry citizens soon gathered, wanting justice for the killing of Rooney. A $500 reward was offered to anyone able to catch the outlaws.

Two days later, officers found Wallace and Woode at their camp five miles south of Victor. They hadn't been hard to find, since they were still wearing their striped prison uniforms. Both were footworn and hungry. Due to public sentiment over the killing of Rooney, the twosome was taken back to the penitentiary hidden in a fruit wagon. Wallace was frightened out of his wits and had to be assisted up some stairs, but he admitted to stabbing Rooney. Lawmen were wise to hide the outlaws, for what happened next would remain a blot on Cañon City's reputation for years.

Within a day, officers also apprehended Tom Reynolds near Florence, but they did not take the same cautions as they had with Wallace and Woode. As the wagon with Reynolds entered town, fire bells began ringing. The wagon got as far as the First Street Bridge before several hundred angry men, who believed Reynolds was Rooney's killer, appeared. The group overpowered the police, took Reynolds and strung him up from the nearest telephone pole. Wagner, meanwhile, was never caught. In the aftermath, Woode was cleared of any wrongdoing. Bob Taylor was released in 1901 for good behavior. He moved to Oklahoma and opened a saloon—where he murdered a deputy marshal in 1907. The killing cost Taylor his own life; he was in turn shot to death by a U.S. marshal.

As for Kid Wallace, who had only a little time left on his original sentence, he received an additional twenty-five years. In 1902, he was part of another escape attempt. This time he was among five prisoners who were discovered out in the prison yard without permission and wisely returned to the jail without a fight. Four years after that, Wallace applied for a pardon. Although it was speculated that the convict could get out as soon as 1914 if he behaved, public sentiment was against the idea. To garner the support he needed, Wallace broke his long-standing refusal to contact his family. A few months

The foreboding wall around the Colorado State Pen in Canon City proved to be only a small challenge to Wallace, Wagner, Reynolds and Woode. *Courtesy Denver Public Library Z6634.*

later, one John Wallace appeared from Nebraska, and it was revealed that that Kid Wallace's real name was Frank Wallace Gaddis. John Wallace was his cousin.

For the first time, the public was given a better glimpse into Kid Wallace's early life. He was born to an equipment engineer, John, and his wife, Ada, in Indiana. Frankie, as the family called him, was the middle child, sandwiched between two sisters. The Gaddises had relocated to Nebraska by 1884 when Ida died. Why Wallace wandered from his family remained a mystery. Not only had he successfully hidden his real name from the authorities, but even John Wallace had no idea the two were related until just after Wallace applied for the pardon. By then, according to newspapers, the boy was nearly deaf, a bit addle-headed and had been relegated to caring for the flower and vegetable gardens at the prison.

Kid Wallace was pardoned in September, and newspapers lambasted Governor Henry Buchtel for doing so. The *Cañon City Daily Record* managed to interview the boy as he waited for the next train out of town. "Am I glad to get out?" he said in a barely audible voice, "Why this is the happiest time I have ever had in my life. But it's all so new and strange. I don't know whether I'm standing on my head or feet." Of his crime, Wallace admitted the F&CC robbery was his first and only crime. "I was young then and thought stealing was easy money," he admitted, "but it's not." The *Daily Record* reporter was clearly impressed by Wallace, calling him a "plain little man" who was almost "child-like." His "subdued manner" genuinely surprised the writer. "Nothing in his ways would picture the desperate prisoner who, knife in hand, fought his way to freedom beyond the penitentiary walls," the reporter wrote. "He will attract no attention on the trains, or anywhere that he may go, for his clothing is plain and simple." Announcing that he was now a Christian, Wallace even shook the reporter's hand and sent a message to the public: "Tell the Cañon City people they won't hear any bad of me. I'm going to live straight from now on."[35]

The last time anyone saw Frank Gaddis, alias Kid Wallace, in Colorado was when he stepped aboard the train and headed to Nebraska. The 1910 census identified him as working at a farm. His draft registration in 1918 shows he had moved to Washington, where he worked as a watchman for a logging company. Sometime after 1920, he married, but his health continued to plague him. By the time he died in 1927 at the young age of forty-nine, nobody even remembered who Kid Wallace, the daring train robber of Colorado, was.

OFFICERS DOWN

Fallen Lawmen of the District

$\mathcal{N}$o history of the wicked side of the Cripple Creek District is complete without a tribute to its many police officers. These men worked hard to wrangle outlaws, con artists, robbers, murderers and a host of many other lawbreakers during the early days of the gold boom and beyond. Many of these men worked long hours for little pay. Some of them valiantly rode, sometimes for miles, to "get their man," as the saying goes. All of them risked their lives in the name of justice. And for nine officers in the district, the end of their watch came much too early.

NIGHT MARSHAL WILLIAM SHEA

The earliest recorded death of an officer in the district was that of Night Marshal William Joseph "Willie" Shea in 1895. He was the second child born to Daniel and Margaret O'Shea in 1864 in Massachusetts (his name is reported in newspapers as Shea, but his family tree spells it O'Shea). In 1870, the family was in Connecticut when Willie's sister died. Perhaps the death of his father in 1891 inspired him to strike out on his own. At some point, Shea landed in Victor, where he was appointed night marshal. His undoing would be Bill Gibson.

Despite being released in the matter of the robbery of the Florence and Cripple Creek train outside of Victor in 1895, William "Bill" Gibson, alias

This undated photo depicts a reenactment of the sort of crime going on in the Cripple Creek District. *Courtesy Cripple Creek District Museum.*

James Gibson, was indeed an outlaw. In fact, he was still a suspect in the robbery of a Wells Fargo Express stage the previous April. Two armed men had accosted the stage between Grassy and Cripple Creek. The driver, Bob Smith, received a terrible beating, and $16,000 in payroll money for the local mines was taken. Two horses were stolen from the stage.

Even as he remained a suspect in the robbery, the early morning hours of August 12 found Gibson in Victor, acting obnoxious and waving a revolver around. Marshal Shea was able to take the gun from him and let him go, but an angry Gibson stomped up to the Strong Mine at the edge of town looking to borrow a gun. When his request was denied, Gibson went to the house of his brother-in-law, where he managed to procure a firearm. He said he only wanted to make Shea return his pistol to him, but what happened next brought his real motive into question. As Gibson walked back downtown, his brother, Pat, went to a local dance house and started raising a ruckus.

Shea soon arrested Pat Gibson for disturbing the peace. The pair were headed to the jail and no more than twenty feet from the dance house when Bill Gibson appeared. Pointing the gun at Shea, he commanded the officer to put up his hands and let his brother go—right as the pistol went off and hit Shea in the stomach. Another officer saw the incident and shot at Gibson but missed. The man escaped as medical help was summoned for Shea. There was no hope for him. Father Downey was summoned from Cripple Creek to administer the victim's last rites as telegraphs were sent to Shea's family in Connecticut. Arrangements were made to ship Shea's body there for burial.

A posse of fifty men formed as Mayor Edwin Ford ordered all Victor saloons to close temporarily, and a $650 reward was offered for Bill Gibson's capture. Everybody was angry, and with good reason: not only had Gibson apparently set up an ambush to kill Shea, but two of his own brothers had once served as sheriff's deputies for Teller County as well. The murderer was soon caught and deposited in jail to await trial. Witnesses testified not only that they saw Gibson shoot Shea in cold blood but also, previous to the incident, Pat Gibson had been going around trying to borrow guns from various people.

On March 1, 1896, Bill Gibson was found guilty of second-degree murder and received a life sentence in the Colorado State Penitentiary. Surprisingly, Pat Gibson was acquitted. Upon being returned to his cell, Bill Gibson tried to overdose on morphine. Doctors revived him, and he lived to begin serving his sentence. Gibson's story does not end there. Beginning in 1898, his own father claimed his son was innocent and began appealing for a pardon. Not one citizen of Victor agreed, but the pleas were kept up for a full five years before Governor James Orman finally granted a pardon. Not surprisingly, Gibson was never heard from again.

CONSTABLE MICHAEL HAYES

Constable Michael Hayes, also of the Victor Police Department, was murdered on June 28, 1897. He had gone to the rural community of Love, some six miles away, simply to serve a court order for rancher Charles Nichols to turn over fifty head of cattle that did not belong to him. Hayes and another man had duly traveled to Love. They first encountered Nichols's wife, who explained the cattle belonged to her. Hayes was walking over to look at the cattle when he saw Nichols. The man was armed with a shotgun and commanded the constable to stop. Then he fired the gun, hitting Michael Hayes square in the chest and killing him instantly.

Nichols headed to Colorado Springs, turned himself in and was given a life sentence at the Colorado State Penitentiary. Just a year later, the murderer

The store at Love, near the home where Constable Michael Hayes lost his life. *Courtesy Cripple Creek District Museum.*

attempted to escape by hiding in the prison stable with a rope in hopes of scaling the wall around the prison but failed. During a second attempt in 1899, Nichols escaped on horseback. The authorities guessed he would be trying to get back to his wife at Love, and that he would not be taken alive. The 1900 census verifies that Nichols was back in prison.

PATROLMAN ELIM T. CLARK

Several years passed before another law officer lost his life, and his story is one of the saddest twists of irony in the history of Cripple Creek. Born in West Virginia, Elim Clark had come west by 1890, when he married Anetta "Nettie" Reed in Colorado Springs. By 1900, the couple had moved to Cripple Creek, where Clark worked in a mine to support Nettie and four young children. Within a year, he joined the Cripple Creek Police Department as a patrolman. His job entailed walking a daily beat on the south end of town.

Following the great fires that burned much of Cripple Creek in 1896, the city installed numbered fireboxes throughout town. The boxes were metal, with a handle on the outside. Inside was a complex system of electrical wires and a telegraphic key. When the handle was cranked, the interior telegraph would relay the box's number to the fire station so the firefighters would know where to go. When Clark noticed a fire on Schidler Street on August 8, 1901, he quickly went to the nearest firebox at the corner of B Street and Thurlow Avenue and pulled the handle.

Most unfortunately, the wires inside the firebox had somehow become crossed, and there was a puddle of water on the ground below. When Clark put his hand to the lever, two thousand volts of electricity shot into his body. Witnesses saw a blue flame shooting from Clark's hand as he cried out, "Take me away—Box 5—Oh, my God," before falling to the ground.[36] He did not survive and was buried in Mt. Pisgah Cemetery. Nettie Clark eventually left Cripple Creek and moved to Denver, where she died in 1922.

NIGHT MARSHAL AUGUSTINE CATE

Augustine Pray Cate was the first lawman to meet his end in the district town of Goldfield. Founded in 1894 as Gold Knob, the name was changed to Goldfield when the city was platted in 1895. Goldfield aspired to be a family town. Modern wooden sidewalks graced the streets, and the Sunday school would eventually become known as the longest-running institution of its kind in the Cripple Creek District. They say that local citizens were far more interested in establishing schools and churches than saloons.

Born in 1854 in Maine, Cate was in Aspen when he married Mary Christina Johnson in 1893. The first of three daughters, Blanche, was born at Goldfield in 1896, and the 1900 census verifies that Augustine worked as a miner. Within two years, he was hired as a night marshal. In the early morning hours of September 21, 1902, Cate was patrolling the city streets when he spied a man coming out of Theodore Stowe's Palace Drug Store. A robbery was in progress.

When the burglar ducked inside the building, Cate instructed witnesses to surround the drugstore and went in through the back door alone. Within two minutes, shots rang out as both the burglar and Cate fired their guns. Cate's bullets missed their mark, but two of the assailant's bullets hit him in the chest. One of those pierced his heart, killing him almost immediately. Additional officers soon arrived and surrounded the building with the impression that the robber was still inside. Within fifteen minutes, however, it was apparent that the man had escaped.

The news made headlines across the state. The *Aspen Democrat* proclaimed that if "the right man was caught he would be lynched without ceremony."[37]

Goldfield as it appeared in 1897. *Courtesy Cripple Creek District Museum CCDM 88.*

A *Rocky Mountain News* article about the incident was headlined "ROPE FOR THUG" in big capital letters.[38] Within a day, the Goldfield City Council offered a reward of $1,000 as Cate's body was taken to Cañon City for burial in Lakeside Cemetery and authorities hunted in vain for his killer. Three days later, three toughs named Kid Rollie, George Bachelder and Jack Gray were arrested. None of them was connected to the murder, but authorities were hoping they might know something. They didn't, and the murderer was never found. Mary Cate eventually moved to Denver, where she died in 1941. Two years after Cate was shot, Isaac Leabo and Chris Miller were appointed temporary constables at Goldfield to keep the peace at a heated election during Cripple Creek's tumultuous labor wars. Both men were shot by Deputy James Warford and subsequently died.[39]

NIGHT PATROLMAN ALBERT B. SMITH

Smith was former resident of Pueblo before moving to Cripple Creek, where he was hired as night patrolman. Just after midnight on November 10, 1908, he was on duty when he witnessed a fight in progress at the Turf Saloon on Bennett Avenue. Proprietor George Goode was fighting with a customer over a woman. Both men were drunk, and the fight, which started inside the saloon, had carried out onto the sidewalk. Goode had a gun in his hand. Smith ran across the street when the men came tumbling out of the saloon. "You will have to stop flashing your gun on the street," he told Goode. In response, Goode sneered, "I'll show you whether or not you will make me put up my gun," and fired directly at Smith's chest.[40] The bullet penetrated his heart, and he died before he hit the ground. Almost immediately, Goode raised the gun to his own head and fired a second shot.

The *Wet Mountain Tribune* of Westcliffe opined that the shooting was indeed "unprovoked, and cold blooded," and asserted that if Goode lived, he would likely be lynched.[41] Sentiments were so strong that an armed guard was placed at Goode's bedside at the St. Nicholas Hospital. The man died on November 12. He was probably buried in the potter's field at Mt. Pisgah Cemetery as Patrolman Smith was given a funeral worthy of a beloved officer. All businesses in town closed while an extensive service was held at the Cripple Creek Elks Lodge. Afterward, a representative of the lodge accompanied Smith's body to Council Grove, Kansas, for burial.

NIGHT MARSHAL HARVEY CALVIN NEESE

Born in 1866 in Pennsylvania, Cal Neese was living in Tennessee when he and several of his brothers decided to move to Cripple Creek in 1895. The men were well liked, and in 1907 Neese married Myrtle Parker in Victor. Neese was still working as a miner when he began moonlighting as night marshal in Cripple Creek during 1911. By the time the Neeses separated in 1920, he was working as night captain full time. All seemed well until the early morning of July 3.

Neese had been called to a skirmish on Bennett Avenue. William Sloan, a former Cripple Creek firefighter, was drunk, threatening to "shoot up the town" and had struck a man named Michael Heslin on the head with the butt of his .45 revolver.[42] Sloan was, in fact, good friends with Neese, but he had just recently been fired from the fire department. Sloan had since "been on a spree" and was drinking excessively. When Neese found him staggering around on Bennett Avenue after hitting Heslin, he probably believed it would be easy to take his friend to jail to sleep it off. "Come along, Bill," he said kindly, "you're under arrest." But instead of complying, Sloan "whipped out his gun and fired one shot at Neese," hitting the officer in the chest.[43] The bullet punctured a lung.

Although Neese was able to grab Sloan's gun, he simultaneously sunk to the ground in the middle of the street. Sloan was arrested, and the fallen officer was taken to the St. Nicholas Hospital, where he died several hours later. His body was taken to Wheat Ridge for burial. Meanwhile, Neese's brother, Arthur, hastened to Cripple Creek and visited Sloan in the Teller County Jail, where he stared the killer down and made a promise: if Sloan ever got out of jail, Neese would kill him. Sloan was convicted and sentenced to life imprisonment at the Colorado State Penitentiary.

Fourteen years later, Colorado governor Edwin Johnson commuted William Sloan's sentence, and he was paroled on May 5, 1934. Determined to carry out his promise, Arthur Neese hastened to the prison and waited, a pistol in each hand, for Sloan to come out. When he saw the prisoner, Neese placed one of the pistols on the ground and dared Sloan to pick it up. The man refused, and his one saving grace was that Neese accidentally dropped his own pistol. The incident ended with both men in tears over the senseless death of a lawman and friend. Sloan even returned to Teller County, where he worked as a farm laborer near the Four Mile District as of the 1940 census. Art Neese died in 1942.

POLICE CHIEF MORRIS DOLAN

Longtime district residents still remember the heroic deed that led to the death of Dolan. Born in Kansas in 1909, he had divorced, remarried and lost one of his young sons by the time he moved to Cripple Creek. By 1940, he had been hired as Cripple Creek's chief of police. Everybody knew Dolan, and everybody liked him. The *Cripple Creek Times-Record* called him "one of the most popular peace officers in the West Pikes Peak Region."[44]

Cripple Creek and its neighboring cities and towns had downsized considerably by the time Dolan lived there. Life was relatively quiet, save for a few bars, some popular restaurants and a handful of shops. So when the Louis Weiner Block, an 1896 building on Bennett Avenue, caught fire, it was huge news. The building was occupied by secondhand store owner Louis Weiner; his wife, Bessie; and their three children, Leslie, Leo, and Louise. Other residents lived in the neighboring buildings.

Everyone was sound asleep when the fire broke out around two o'clock on the morning of August 23. As the fire alarm sounded, everybody woke up and ran outside. But when Dolan, who was also head of the Cripple Creek Fire Department, arrived on the scene, he learned that a child, possibly fifteen-year-old Leo Weiner or his seven-year-old sister, Louise, might still be inside the building. The chief donned a gas mask and dashed into the burning structure. Several minutes later, Victor fire chief Armour Olson and firefighter Henry "June" Hack arrived and were told that Dolan was still in the building. Olson and Hack quickly put on their own gas masks, entered the building, and found Dolan unconscious in a second-floor room filled with smoke. The rest of the building was empty. Olson and Hack dragged Dolan from the building and took him to St. Nicholas Hospital, where he died from smoke inhalation. A hero's funeral was held for him at Mt. Pisgah Cemetery.

Sheriff Cecil Markley's investigation of the fire revealed that it had been set by William Hailey, a Cripple Creek firefighter who had already been suspected of several fires around town, as well as in Leadville. Hailey ultimately admitted that he "had an uncontrollable desire to set fires since he was seven years old."[45] He was sentenced to sixty years in the state

Young Bud Peiffer (*right*) and a friend view the burned out Weiner Building. The Peiffers were early settlers in Cripple Creek. *Courtesy Cripple Creek District Museum.*

penitentiary at Cañon City, was paroled after ten years and wound up in Denver, where he died in 1986. Back in Cripple Creek, people would not forget that Police Chief Dolan had lost his life in the fire—but it was not until much later that someone decided to recognize his heroism.

In 1999, June Hack happened to attend a memorial service alongside Colorado State Patrol officer Keith Dameron. Hack told Dameron the whole story of Morris Dolan and his heroic death. When the online Colorado Law Enforcement Memorial was formed some years later, Dameron tracked down Dolan's daughter for details of the story and researched old newspapers to find out more. In 2012, Dolan's name also was added to the National Law Enforcement Officers Memorial in Washington, D.C. The *Pikes Peak Courier* published an article about it, speaking for so many by noting, "Sometimes it takes a while for a hero to be acknowledged."[46]

COUNTESS DOUGLAS McPHERSON

*I*n a time when most male pioneers in the high mining camps across the West found themselves without female company, life could be quite lonely. Although they certainly mingled, drank and played cards together, the male species rarely found much else in the way of entertainment. If a musician was handy, there might be the occasional dance, with participants taking turns being the "female" partner. In cases where men occupied a cabin together, they inevitably shared such stereotypical women's work as cooking and cleaning. Miners' homes were often small, to the effect that in a cramped cabin, it just sometimes made sense to share one bed instead of two that would just take up more room. Today, one of history's biggest secrets is that some men quietly shared their affection for each other as well. That is where Douglas C. McPherson comes in.

Born in Scotland in 1874, McPherson immigrated to America in 1888. He first appeared in Denver in about 1895. He eventually relocated to the district town of Altman, where he found work as a miner and rented a room north of Baldwin Avenue. Within a year, McPherson had ingratiated himself with the El Paso County commissioners, who appointed him as one of three election judges for the Altman precinct. Everybody seemed to like him, and he was quite the social butterfly. In 1898, the *Victor Record* reported, "Mr. and Mrs. George McMillan entertained Mr. Douglas MacPherson [*sic*] and Robert Cameron at a 5 o'clock dinner last Sunday."[47] A month later, McPherson made the papers

A group of men dancing with one another, in lieu of having any women present. *Wikimedia Commons.*

again: "Samuel R. Johnesse gave a delightful card party last Saturday evening to a number of invited guests. Rare cut flowers ornamented the tables, and refreshments were served to Mr. and Mrs. Frederick W. Grace, Mr. and Mrs. J. S. Murphy, Miss Regina Neville, Messrs. Daniel Murphy, Douglas McPherson and A. Baxter. An enjoyable time was had."[48]

The 1900 census verified that "Dugless" McPherson was a naturalized citizen who could read and write. He shared his cabin northwest of the Pharmacist Mine with his "pardner," William Millar, a fellow Scotsman who also immigrated to America in 1888. Both were employed at the Pharmacist. Whatever the relationship between McPherson and Millar was, it appears the people of Altman thoroughly enjoyed their company. No descriptions were offered about Millar, but McPherson was noted as having "long flowing curls."[49] He was also occasionally prone to crossdressing. That might have been why the *Cripple Creek Daily Press* especially took an interest in McPherson and his social activities. The newspaper's "Altman Briefs" column followed McPherson quite closely, noting the colorful outfits he wore to the theater and how he looked after cutting his long hair short. Once, while sorting ore at the nearby Pinto Mine, McPherson's foot was injured. The paper reported about that too. More would come in June 1901, when the *Daily Press* reported, perhaps tongue-in-cheek, that McPherson intended to leave for New York City, where he expected to attend acting school.

Although the news articles about McPherson came dangerously close to poking fun at the man, the people of Altman appear to have accepted him for who he was. One article, on July 14, called him "Countess McPherson" when he attended a local festival. This time, the *Daily Press* reported how he "fell dead in love with the female impersonator in the German Village Thursday night and wanted to stay until the show was over and escort her home." McPherson's male friends objected to that idea and "finally dragged him away by force."[50] The "boys" referenced in the article were likely McPherson's fellow miners, who apparently wanted to make sure he did not miss work the next morning. There is nothing to suggest that the men outright objected to the idea of McPherson taking another man home.

Indeed, McPherson's fellow miners had good reason to like him, no matter his sexual preferences. In addition to being an electoral judge, he also was a card-carrying member of the Western Federation of Miners'

This miner's cabin on display at the Cripple Creek District Museum illustrates how men might share quarters, including the same bed. *Author's collection.*

Free Coinage Union Np. 19. When he and another man named Billy Mercer hosted a dinner party at their cabin for some friends in late July, the *Daily Press* reported it simply as a matter of keeping tabs on the social events of the district.[51] Sometime after that, however, Douglas McPherson disappeared from record in the district. He may have returned to Denver, where one "Dug" McPherson was employed as a barber for P.L. Lavell in 1901 and lived at a lodging house on Market Street.

William Millar, meantime, remained in the district. By 1902, he had moved to Victor, where he rented a room in a house on North Fourth Street and worked at the Independence Mine. A few years later, he fell ill. While he recuperated at Victor's Red Cross Hospital, Millar fell in love with his nurse, Ida Clark, and married her. Fortuitously, Millar also discovered he was heir to several wealthy estates in his homeland. The last anyone knew of the happy couple they had left for Scotland. Like Douglas MacPherson, they never returned to the district.

THE HARLOT WHO BURNED DOWN CRIPPLE CREEK

*S*ex work has a long history in Colorado. Shortly after the state's first gold boom during the late 1850s, women of the night infiltrated the Centennial State knowing that where there were men, there was likely to be gold, or silver, or some other valuable form of trade. By the time of the gold boom in the Cripple Creek District, Colorado's harlots were quite seasoned. They knew that the budding district provided ample opportunities to set up a brothel. Getting into the game early was essential, before reformers, church women and law officials had a chance to control and abate the women's livelihoods. Dance hall girls and prostitutes were already in Cripple Creek by April 1892, when a fire began on the south side of Bennett Avenue. Between seven and a dozen buildings burned, including some saloons. Notable is that a dance hall girl, Lutie Cook, reportedly rescued two small children by handing them down from the second-floor window of the Arcade Restaurant.

Cook was not the only dance hall girl in town. By 1893, Cripple Creek, as well as the communities of Altman, Barry and Victor, was home to dance hall girls and prostitutes. One of the first mentions of the ladies was made during the labor strikes of 1893, when the red-light women were among those to vacate the entire town of Altman in a protest against local mine owners. "The entire population of the camp packed up their effects," reported the *Aspen Daily Times* on February 7, "and a motley procession was formed, including miners, saloonkeepers and their outfits, merchants with their stocks and the denizens of the brothels. The hilarious cavalcade moved to Cripple Creek and within a few hours the camp was deserted."[52]

As the city in which most of the budding mining millionaires spent their time, Cripple Creek was the best place for wayward women to settle. By March 1893, there were five brothels situated throughout the city.

CRIPPLE CREEK'S EARLY HOUSES OF PROSTITUTION, MARCH 1893

Block and Lot	Identified As	Description	Address Then	Address Today
B10, L7	"Female Boarding"	Two-story brothel with tent in back	326 Eaton Avenue	326 E. Eaton Avenue
B15, L12	"Female Boarding"	One-story brothel between Third and Fourth Streets	1518 Carr Avenue	City Hall parking lot
B16, L40	"Ill Fame"	One-story brothel between Bennett and Carr Avenues	811 Third Street	Imperial Hotel
B22, Lot29	"Female Boarding"	Two-story brothel with cabin on back of lot	317 Myers Avenue	Parking Lot
B23, L12	"Female Boarding"	Small one-story brothel	406 Bennett Avenue	Double Eagle Hotel and Casino[53]

As churches and proper womenfolk gradually settled in town, both strongly objected to the wayward women on Bennett Avenue. They were hanging out of the second-floor windows of the saloons or snatching men's hats and running into such places as a means of luring their victims inside. Their singing in the tippling houses and dance halls could be heard on the streets. They also seemed to have no issues about sweeping past respectable women on the sidewalks and sneering at those who would look down their high-toned noses at them. In an effort to make everyone happy, Sheriff Hiram Wilson approached the wayward ladies in November 1894. If they would move to the corner of Third Street and Myers Avenue and conduct their business east of that spot, Wilson promised, the demimonde would remain unmolested by the law. But the ladies really had no choice in the matter. "Positive orders have been issued by the city council for the immediate vacation of the property on the corner of Myers [A]venue and 4th Street by the prostitutes now in occupation," the *Cripple Creek Morning Journal* announced. "The gay and festive inhabitants of this quarter have been notified to move and will be ejected by summary process if the order of the board is not immediately obeyed."[54]

Myers Avenue between Third and Fourth Streets was soon abuzz with activity. There were drinking houses, gambling joints, variety theaters and enough shops that the ladies on the row could easily work around new rules, such as being allowed on Bennett Avenue only one day a week for their shopping needs. The proper ladies of Cripple Creek, meanwhile, wisely designated that day as washday, to avoid running into the scarlet women. All was well until a dry, cold and windy day on Saturday, April 25, 1896. Just that morning, a local newspaper wrote of how Cripple Creek's up-and-coming fire department had just purchased brand-new hoses. A newly built reservoir above town assured everyone that any fire could quickly be extinguished. Everyone was going about their business. And none of them seemed to notice a disgruntled man who was marching down Myers Avenue with a scowl on his face. His name was Otto Floto.

Born in Ohio, the thirty-three-year-old Floto had developed a fondness for promoting the popular sport of boxing. His career began in Chicago, where he managed various pugilists while writing sports columns for a local newspaper. The trouble was that Floto was hot-tempered. In San Francisco in 1894, he and boxer Jack McAuliffe were pulled into court for beating the daylights out of one Young Mitchell. Eight months later, in Anaconda, Montana, Floto and Charles Marion of the Bank Exchange Saloon solicited

Early Myers Avenue was initially intended to be a respectable business street. *Courtesy Cripple Creek District Museum A 82 22.*

one hundred laborers to march in a local parade in exchange for pay and supper. Yet those who showed up were told there were too many of them, and the promised pay was cut to fifty cents and no supper. When the disgruntled men started dispersing, Marion threatened to evict those who were sleeping on the floor in a room above his saloon, while Floto threatened to have them all fired from their jobs. Some of the men agreed to march, but when they came for their money the next morning, they were told there was none to be had.

Floto was in Denver in April 1895 when he was arrested for committing perjury and jumping bond in Butte, Montana. The governor of Montana refused to extradite him, however, and Floto wisely stayed on the down-low for a while. A year later, he was in Cripple Creek, quietly managing the Cripple Creek Bill Posting Company on South Second Street. Floto lived on Warren Avenue. Myers Avenue lay in between the two places. There were now around thirty houses of prostitution, saloons and dance halls along Myers.

So many women worked on Myers Avenue that many of their names have been lost to history. Had it not been for the great Cripple Creek fires of 1896, Jennie Larue's name may never have been mentioned in print. Scant documentation about her reveals only that she was born in Canada in 1869, came to America as a child in 1880 and had previously married, and divorced, in Leadville circa 1890. Her maiden or married name was Reid;

Jennie Larue was just her working moniker. Now she lived on the second floor of the Central Dance Hall, and Otto Floto was her man.

On April 25, Jennie was in her room, ironing near the warmth of a small gasoline stove. For some reason, Floto was in a fit as he marched up the stairs to Jennie's room, and a heated argument ensued. That's when, depending on the source, Jennie threw a lamp at Floto and/or the couple stumbled into the little stove, which tipped over. Alternatively, they may have been in the back of the dance hall when they bumped into the stove, which belonged to a Mr. Jones who ran the lunch counter. However it happened, the gasoline spilled as little rivers of flames spread over the floor and quickly grew.

As smoke began billowing out of the Central Dance Hall, the fire department rushed to the scene with a hose cart and attempted to connect the new hoses to the closest hydrant. If only someone had checked to make sure the nozzles were compatible with the plugs on the hydrants! Alas, they were not. The fire spread to the Union Dance Hall and Casey's Second-Hand Store on either side of the Central before the hoses were jimmied onto the hydrants, but there was so little water pressure that some of them had to be disconnected and a couple of them broke. The fire department in Victor could see the smoke and rushed over to help. The reservoir above town was depleted before the fire was out, but at last the flames were quelled.

Over seven blocks of downtown Cripple Creek were left smoldering. Gone was the red-light district, as were nearly all buildings along Bennett, Myers and Warren Avenues between Second and Fifth Streets. Amazingly, nobody was killed. In the coming days, newspapers all over America covered the fire. A few of them named Jennie. "Dawson City's Belle Mitchell has joined Chicago's Mrs. O'Leary and Cripple Creek's Jennie LaRue in the list of women who became famous as fire builders," snarked Leadville's *Herald Democrat* in the months afterward.[55] Floto's name was never mentioned. And Jennie's name would soon be forgotten, as a second fire erupted in Cripple Creek just four days after the first one.

On April 29 a survivor of the fire, the Portland Hotel, went up in flames at the southwest corner of Second Street and Myers Avenue. Built in 1894 as the Pikes Peak Hotel, the building was once a grand, two-story affair containing a large kitchen and dining room; a saloon, a billiards parlor and offices on the first floor; and rooms on the second floor. The hotel was initially considered first class. After the manager, Mrs. C. Butterfield, left in 1895, however, the hotel's name was changed to the Portland and was soon showing much wear and tear.

The most accepted story of how the fire began is that someone spilled some grease while cooking in the hotel's grimy kitchen, and it caught the wall behind it on fire. Chef Frank Angel ran from the building. Waitress Bessie Kelly told officials that when she saw the flames, she shouted "Fire!" throughout the hotel. Bartender C.W. Kelly heard Bessie hollering and wasn't too concerned at first. Then, he said, "I looked up and saw the flames shooting through the six-inch stove pipe hole in the wall next to the toilet room. I took the money and left the room, nothing else being saved." The building was evacuated, but some employees upstairs barely escaped.[56]

Strong winds fanned the flames, which spread quickly. There being no fire bell, someone fired off six shots into the air to warn everyone. The fire department rushed to the scene, but the reservoir above town was still dry from the previous conflagration. Within fifteen minutes, the Portland collapsed into a heap of burning rubble as more buildings burned, including the El Paso Lumber Yard. The Harder Grocery Store had seven hundred pounds of dynamite stored away and exploded as the boilers in the Palace Hotel at Second Street and Bennett Avenue erupted, sending flames one hundred feet into the air.

The only thing people could do was load whatever they could into wagons and get out of harm's way. Barrels and boxes and furnishings were scattered in the streets. One witness told of a man who was so confused

Smoke billows into the air during Cripple Creek's second fire. *Courtesy Cripple Creek District Museum A82-346.*

Myers Avenue rebuilt after the fires to provide all-new saloons, theaters, dance halls and brothels. *Courtesy Cripple Creek District Museum.*

that he ran out on the landing from his second-story room and heaved a heavy mirror over the handrail but then carefully carried a flatiron down the stairs and set it on the ground next to the shattered glass. Some unscrupulous wagon owners tried to charge one hundred dollars to haul goods to the edge of town as the fire department began blowing up buildings in a desperate effort to stop the flames from spreading. When the flames were extinguished several hours later, fifteen city blocks, nearly one hundred businesses and three hundred homes, were reduced to ashes. "Cripple Creek Doomed," the *Boulder Daily Camera* stated flatly in its evening edition.[57] The paper was not far off, for most of the town looked like a war zone as night fell. Only the homes on the north and west sides of town and the Midland Terminal Depot and Colorado Trading & Transfer Company on the east side survived. Looters and thieves ran amuck as police and do-gooders chased after them.

Cripple Creek, if nothing else, remained resilient. Thanks to mining millionaire Winfield Scott Stratton, trains from Colorado Springs began bringing a wealth of tents, blankets, food and other items to help the homeless. The towns around the district and as far away as Florence opened their homes to evacuees. The local mines closed long enough for the miners to help clear out the debris, and even the First National Bank managed to set up temporary quarters in a burned-out warehouse to give pay advances. Within days, the city of Cripple Creek was being rebuilt.

The Sells Floto Circus remained independent until 1921, when it was absorbed by the American Circus Corporation. *Library of Congress.*

Surprisingly, neither Jennie Larue nor Otto Floto left town. Six months later, on October 20, the couple was married right there in Cripple Creek. Floto resumed promoting local boxing matches, sometimes traveling as far as Nevada with client Bob Fitzsimmons for matches in Carson City. It was there that Floto met Harry Tammen, publisher of the *Denver Post*. Tammen was so enamored of Floto's unusual name that he decided to use it for a performing circus act he owned. He also offered Floto a sportswriting job. Shortly after his return to Cripple Creek, Floto and his bride moved to Denver.

Although Floto was never personally involved with Tammen's Sells-Floto Circus, he probably enjoyed being associated with it in name. He began working for the Colorado Athletic Club, and the 1900 census confirmed he was the sports editor for the *Post*. The Flotos had no children and never would; in November 1906, they divorced after nine years of what was likely a bumpy marriage. Floto remarried to a bareback rider from Sells-Floto circus named Kitty Kruger and remained a well-known figure around Denver for many years. He died in 1929 and is buried in Fairmount Cemetery. Jennie, meanwhile, disappeared from records altogether. She is remembered today only as the floozy who burned down Cripple Creek.

THE HOLE IN THE WALL GANG'S HIDEOUT

There is little doubt that Bob Lee likely disapproved of his own lifestyle. Yet here he was, planted in Cripple Creek by his own cousins on behalf of the infamous Hole in the Wall Gang. Lee was a cousin to the outlaw gang via Harvey Logan, better known as the notorious Kid Curry. Logan and his brothers Johnny and Lonnie, all of whom were raised with Lee in Missouri, would later become an integral part of the gang. And if not for Lee's arrest, Cripple Creek might never have been known as a one-time hideout for the outlaws.

Lee's story begins with his cousins: James Logan, Denver Henry "Hank" Logan, John Logan, Loranzo "Lonnie" Dow Logan and Harvey Alexander Logan. The boys, along with their sister Arda, were all just children when they came to live with Lee's family in Dodson, Missouri, after their father, William Logan, died. A short time later, their mother, Eliza Logan, also died. Lee's parents, Hiram and Lizzie Lee, raised the Logan boys as their own until about 1886. By that year, the Logan brothers (except for James) and Lee, along with a former robber named Jim Thornhill, were running a horse ranch in Montana, just south of Landusky. Notable is that Lee and his cousins were already going by an alias, using the last name of Curry.

When Harvey, Lonnie and Thornhill shot neighbor Powell "Pike" Landusky to death during a dispute in 1894, they officially became outlaws. With Lee in tow, the Logans fled to Johnson County, Wyoming, where Harvey soon formed the Logan Brothers Gang and began running with the likes of Butch Cassidy, Harry Longabaugh (the Sundance Kid), Will Carver,

Elzy Lay and others of the Hole in the Wall Gang. Lee didn't seem like much of an outlaw. He had a studious look and was sometimes referred to as "stocky." William Pinkerton of Pinkerton Detective Agency would later describe Lee as "a very absent minded fellow, a very peculiar fellow."[58]

Lee eventually returned to the family home and stayed there for a couple of years. In 1897, however, he wrote Harvey Logan that he wanted "to get away from" his mother in Dodson. Logan wrote back with instructions for Lee to go to Harlem, Montana. Logan was waiting for him. "My God that kid has grown tall," Logan remembered thinking when he saw his cousin. "I hardly know him."[59] Lee was also about as green as they came. Logan recalled how he and saloon owner George Bowles spent some money to get the boy "out of his city duds and introduce[ed] him to the girlie houses."[60] The three then traveled to Hole in the Wall, the gang's hideout in northern Wyoming. Longabaugh set about teaching Lee the fine art of cowboy and outlaw living. But the boy was so slow to catch on that when the gang robbed a Wyoming stagecoach during August 1897, they only used Lee as a lookout.

Lee may not have been adept at robbing people, but he was a great poker player. He easily outbluffed and won hands over the others at Hole in the Wall—a knack that was not lost on Longabaugh. "Look, Bob gambles better than anything else," he told Logan. "Why don't you set him up in a gambling house somewhere? Cripple Creek, Colorado—that's a good place. We don't have any connections in Colorado. We might need a location down there some day."[61] Logan agreed.

A month or so later, Logan and Lee traveled to Cripple Creek. The boomtown was teeming with gamblers and saloons. The pair built an inconspicuous one-room cabin on the edge of town and visited several gambling houses. Prospects were good. Lee began playing cards, and his instinct as a natural-born winner was not lost on the table bosses. Before long, he had a job running a poker table while Logan took a trip to the McCoy Ranch near Cotopaxi. The McCoys were a rough bunch, carrying on their own illegal operations that included the 1891 robbery of a Denver and Rio Grande train near their ranch. Logan was hoping to pull some jobs with the McCoys, and he visited them before returning to Hole in the Wall.

Lee's job in Cripple Creek included making money, as well as dispersing it to the gang as needed. Just before he and Logan set up their Cripple Creek hideout, the Hole in the Wall Gang attempted to rob a bank in Belle Fourche, South Dakota. But they bungled the job, and Logan was among those outlaws who were caught in September. Lee later remembered receiving a letter from Deadwood law firm McLaughlin and Temple. The attorneys

Harvey Logan and his common-law wife, Annie Rogers, pictured around the time Bob Lee joined the Hole in the Wall Gang. *Library of Congress.*

"wrote to me that a man was in jail at Deadwood for the Belle Fourche bank robbery and wanted financial help," Lee explained. "The lawyers said the man would not give a name, but they described him and I knew it was Harvey Logan. I did not send any money."[62]

Logan was out of jail by the spring of 1898, when he visited Cripple Creek again under the alias of Harve Wright. He and Lee took a trip to go see the McCoys a second time. The pair staked a placer claim along the Arkansas River so that anyone who happened along the road would think they were just two prospectors looking for gold. Lee also worked briefly on a claim owned by Judd Spencer. When nothing came of either the gold or McCoy prospects, the men returned to Cripple Creek. Lee got a job running the faro table at the Board of Trade saloon while Logan returned to Hole in the Wall. Lee would later remember that Longabaugh, under the tongue-in-cheek alias of Frank Scramble, came to visit him at the Board of Trade several times. "I was introduced to him by a big German teamster or express man whose name I do not remember," Lee said.[63]

Harvey Logan continued visiting Lee regularly. In April 1899, he told Lee that the gang planned to rob the Union Pacific Railroad's Overland Flyer in Wyoming, and they needed his help. Per Logan's instructions, Lee met up with Lonnie Logan in Montana and procured some getaway horses for the robbery. On June 2, the robbery took place near Wilcox, Wyoming. When the railroad express guard, Charles Woodcock, refused to open the door, the robbers responded by packing dynamite around the whole train car and setting it off. The car was blown to bits as a cloud of banknotes fluttered into the air. This well-known incident in outlaw history was forever immortalized in the 1969 movie *Butch Cassidy and the Sundance Kid*.

Newspapers would reveal that some $40,000 was "taken in the form of uncut sheets of large-size National Bank Notes being shipped by the Treasury to The National Bank of Montana" in Helena. Other loot included $500 in cash, four Elgin watches, four gold "hunting cases," a gold vest chain, nineteen scarf pins and twenty-nine pairs of cuff buttons.[64] Spending the cash would not be a problem, but the bank notes were missing the required signatures from bank officials. Was Lee there to divide the spoils? Nobody knows to this day, but Lonnie Logan probably was. Soon after the robbery, he returned to Harlem and began openly spending money, dressing like a dandy and flirting with women. He also purchased a half interest in George Bowles's Club Saloon. The name of the saloon was changed to Bowles and Curry. By September, Lee had traveled from Cripple Creek and was working there as a bartender.

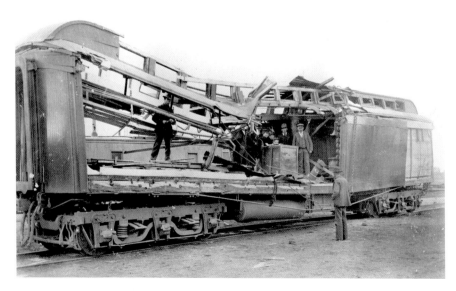

The Union Pacific train at Wilcox, Wyoming, after it was blown to smithereens. *Courtesy Wyoming State Archives #21457.*

By November 19, Montana banks were reporting they had received some of the banknotes from the Wilcox robbery. Some had apparently been forged and cashed in Harlem. Later, Lee would recall that Lonnie Logan, who still owed George Bowles $300, told him that he intended to cash in $500 worth of the banknotes—in his cousin's name. "I knew nothing whatever of the robbery at this time," Lee claimed, "and the reason he wanted the money sent in my name was because he did not want Bowles to know he had any money. I never saw but two of these bills, one that Lonnie changed in the saloon and one that he gave to his wife to give to the Sister Superior of the convent for the keeping of his child."[65]

Just after New Years, Pinkerton detective W.B. Sayers visited Harlem. Logan and Lee got wind of it, quickly sold their saloon to one George Ringwald and left town.[66] Although the *Phillips County News* in Malta reported the pair had "conducted themselves in a peaceable and law-abiding manner, almost exemplary," one of them, the paper confirmed, was wanted for his part in the Wilcox robbery.[67] As the paper puzzled over how those nice "Curry" boys could be mixed up in the robbery, Logan and Lee escaped to Cripple Creek. Jim Thornhill would later recall that Logan visited his ranch along the way, telling him, "We got to hit the trail." Logan gave Thornhill some money, telling him that Ringwald would "bring $700 more to you soon. When you get it, Jimmer, send it in a package to Frank Miller, general delivery, Cripple Creek, Colorado. I'm going there with Bob. He's got a hangout in Cripple Creek."[68]

When the outlaws returned to Cripple Creek, Lee found a job dealing cards at the Antlers Saloon while Logan busied himself visiting the post office every morning looking for Thornhill's package. Before long, he roused the suspicions of postmaster Danny Sullivan. When Logan left for Kansas in early February, Sullivan contacted the authorities. Pinkerton agents hastened to Cripple Creek. Now, both Logan and Lee were suspects in the Wilcox affair, and Sullivan knew where Lee worked. Later, Pinkerton superintendent James McFarland noted, "Were it not for Sullivan assisting the Agency in the manner that he did it might have been years before we would have been able to locate Bob Lee."[69]

Logan, meanwhile, had wisely taken the back roads and remote trails back to Kansas, working small jobs along the way rather than risk cashing another bank note. Upon reaching his aunt Lee's house, however, he made the fatal mistake of spending another stolen bank note at the nearby community of Dodson. The note was immediately traced, and in the early morning hours of February 28, 1900, six Pinkerton agents arrived at the Lee house. Logan fled into the yard, and after a brief exchange of gunfire, he was killed by the agents. A search of the house turned up some letters from Lee to his mother. They were postmarked Cripple Creek.

Until now, the authorities were not certain of who was at the Wilcox robbery. They never would be. Lonnie Logan was the first robber caught. With him dead, that left only Lee, alias Bob Curry—the least likely suspect of all. Pinkerton detectives sent a telegraph to lawmen in Cripple Creek on March 1. Lee was working at Antlers that evening when Undersheriff J.D. Harrigan, Deputy Matt Deering and Deputy Joe O'Brien walked in. *The Cripple Creek Morning Times-Citizen* told the story of what happened next: "The undersheriff walked straight up to him and asked if his name was Bob Lee. Curry looked up quickly and, with a suspicious gleam in his eyes, asked: 'What is it to you?' 'Well never mind,' replied Harrington [*sic*], 'you're the man I want. You are under arrest.'"[70]

Not until they reached the jail did Harrigan tell Lee he was wanted for the Wilcox robbery. "Curry shut up like a clam and has since refused to talk," said the *Morning Times-Citizen*. A search of the outlaw revealed only a pearl-handled six-shooter "of the most approved pattern," as well as a valise containing newspaper clippings about the Wilcox robbery.[71] Lee hadn't a cent on him. News of his arrest soon reached the Hole in the Wall Gang, and key is that in discussing Lee's arrest with Butch Cassidy, Harvey Logan stated, "Hell, he and Lonny [*sic*] didn't rob anybody."[72] The robbers apparently knew that Lee was not present at Wilcox. Meanwhile, the *Morning Times-Citizen* capitalized on Lee's arrest, claiming that the "Curry Brothers" had been skulking around the district since 1894 and that the outlaws' friends were still in town.

Lee was taken to the jail at Laramie, but it was two months before William Pinkerton interviewed him. "At first Lee was not inclined to talk to us and for nearly an hour and a half he said nothing, except to reply to questions directed to him and it looked for a time he was not going to tell anything," Pinkerton wrote in his report. When he did finally speak, Lee stated he knew nothing about the Wilcox robbery except what Lonnie Logan had told him. He did identify three of the robbers: Harvey Logan, the man he knew as Frank Scramble and a third, unidentified man. "One has got to be very careful in getting any statements from him," Pinkerton wrote, "because he wavers so much in his statements."[73]

At Lee's trial on May 25, he was represented by attorneys R.W. Brockonn of Cheyenne, Blake Woodson of Kansas City, and J. Maurice

Finn, the spunky little lawyer who was employed by several mine owners in the Cripple Creek District. It was Finn who opened his defense by stating that Lee was not even in Wyoming at the time of the Wilcox robbery. Two dozen witnesses testified that Lee was in Black Hawk, Colorado, on June 2, 1899, and that he didn't leave there until late June or early July. Others also testified to his presence in Montana and Colorado during the time of the robbery. But those claims were countered by others who remembered seeing Lee handling the stolen banknotes in Harlem and his association with the Logan boys.

Finn was a virtual whirlwind in the courtroom during his closing arguments, shouting out how the witness testimonies had exonerated his client from any wrongdoing and reminding the jury of Lee's many "good points." The *Cheyenne Leader* noted that by the time Finn was finished, he was a bit sweaty and "quite exhausted."[74] It was all for naught. Lee was found guilty and sentenced to ten years of hard labor at the Wyoming State Penitentiary in Rawlins. He was so overwhelmed by the verdict that he fell into his chair and could not stand up again.

Lee's sentence began on May 31 as Pinkerton agent Frank Murray notified Marshal Hadsell that agent J.C. Fraser was in Cripple Creek looking for Harvey Logan, Frank Scramble and "the big Dutchman" who had introduced Scramble to Lee. "Wish Bob Lee had better memory of this Scramble party," Murray corresponded on June 8. "I wonder if Bob could say whether Scramble is "Kid" Longbaugh [*sic*] or not." A few days later, Murray wrote again. "I wish we knew more about this Frank Scramble and wish we could ascertain whether or not he is 'Kid' Longbaugh. We do not like guessing at it and yet it seems he must be.... We have not got the least thing, not the slightest trace of the big German or any one up there who ever knew Frank Scramble and no one who seems to remember Harvey Logan."[75]

Pinkerton superintendent James McParland, meanwhile, was unhappy with Undersheriff Harrigan for his solo claim to the $1,000 reward offered for Lee's arrest. "You will note," fumed McParland to U.S. District Attorney T.F. Burke, "that in the written portion of [Harrigan's] application, first, in making this arrest the name of Daniel M. Sullivan is left out; second, that Mr. Harrigan claims the entire reward; third, Harrigan states that at his request Daniel M. Sullivan located Lee at a certain gambling-house table dealing poker." McParland concluded that Harrigan lied on the application and wanted the reward for himself. "Each and every officer connected with the arrest of Lee claims an equal portion of this reward,"

J. Maurice Finn, the colorful attorney who defended Bob Lee and a host of other outlaws in the Cripple Creek District. *Courtesy Cripple Creek District Museum.*

Bob Lee scowls at the camera at the Wyoming State Penitentiary, where he spent time for a crime he likely didn't commit. *Courtesy Wyoming State Archives #491.*

McParland ranted. A copy of his letter was sent to Marshal Hadsell with the comment that Harrigan's move "is decidedly the most underhanded thing that I have ever seen."[76]

In another letter to Hadsell in February 1901, Judd Spencer, Lee's former employer at Cotopaxi, rallied for pardoning the man. Most interesting is that Spencer made mention of another Wilcox suspect in Cripple Creek, described as "a man about six feet tall, heavy set, dark complected, and went under the name of Crumble or Crumbley."[77] Whether the man was Sherman Crumley, the small-time robber whose antics were well known around the district, will likely never be known. Lee remained the only link the authorities had to the Wilcox robbery. Whenever the Hole in the Wall Gang committed another crime, he was grilled for details.

Finally, in 1902, an anguished Lee wrote to Hadsell himself. "You have told me that you know I wasn't in the Robry which I was convicted for and know and believe that you are more therbay convinced you have promest me and my frindes that you would do what you could to arrang helping me out of my trouble [*sic*]," Lee pleaded. "I wouldn't of asked any favors of Gov only from what that I have bin promest and I believe that you ar therebay convinced of my unjust punishment [*sic*]."[78] But Lee was still in prison when Harvey Logan died during a shootout near Parachute, Colorado, in 1904. The following year, he was finally released for good behavior. He was still in Wyoming during 1906 when Buffalo Bill Cody's Wild West came through. The performances were to include a train robbery reenactment, and Cody personally asked Lee if he wanted to participate. He was turned down.

Lee eventually returned to Missouri, where he married Minnie Miller in Kansas City in 1912. Two years later, he succumbed to Bright's disease. His obituary in the *Kansas City Star* noted that Lee was a great-nephew of his namesake, General Robert E. Lee. The writers did not mention his time with the Hole in the Wall Gang, but today a sign reading "Robert Lee member of Butch Cassidy Wild Bunch [*sic*]" can be seen at his grave.

TEDDY ROOSEVELT'S
PROBLEM CHILD

*O*f the hundreds of scam artists who once targeted the Cripple Creek District, Benjamin Franklin "Ben" Daniels must certainly take the cake. Born in Illinois in 1852, Cripple Creek's future bad boy had a most difficult childhood. He lost most of his family, including his mother, to cholera in 1854. By 1865, his father had remarried. The family was farming in Kansas when young Daniels struck out and headed for Texas. He had decided he wanted to be a cowboy.

Daniels had a commanding presence: he was over six feet in height, with black hair, black eyes and "enormous strength."[79] By 1879, he was in Wyoming when he was convicted of stealing army mules. When he got out of jail, Daniels returned to Kansas and took a job hunting buffalo before moving to Dodge City by about 1884. He quickly became known among the dance halls, saloons and gambling houses and was appointed assistant marshal under Marshal William Tilghman in April 1885. Just under a year later, however, an all-new city administration was voted into city hall and Daniels lost his job. Why did this happen? Because Daniels was among a dozen "saloon druggists" who had been arrested for dispensing liquor while a "prohibitory law" was in effect.[80]

Daniels had no sooner been relieved from the police force when he killed a man. A news article told the story:

> *On last Thursday evening at about six o'clock, a shooting scrape took place on the south side of the railroad on the sidewalk in front of Utterback's*

hardware store, two doors west of Ed Julian's restaurant, the latter gentleman being the victim in the affray; and his antagonist, ex-assistant city marshal Ben Daniels. Four shots were fired, all by Daniels, all of which took effect on Julian. While Julian was found to be armed, he however, did not get to fire a shot; there is much diversity of opinion in the matter, some claiming it to have been a deliberate murder, while others assert it to have been justifiable. The evidence taken at the preliminary trial does not fully sustain either.[81]

Daniels was confident he would not be held for killing Julian. While awaiting his case to come up, the alleged murderer held a grand party at his El Dorado Saloon in September that soon spilled out the doors and spread throughout the whole town. Daniels was like that. He could make a mess of things and somehow come out smelling like a rose. In November, shortly after selling his saloon, Daniels was indeed acquitted of Julian's murder. Ever the wanderer, he made trips to Kansas City, as well as Colorado. In January 1887, the *Bent County Register* in Lamar noted that Daniels "thinks of coming here to live."[82]

Daniels was in Independence, Missouri, when he managed to find someone to marry him. Her name was Anna Laura Broaddus, and the two were united in matrimony in March 1887. Sure enough, the newlyweds soon relocated to Lamar, where, by 1888, Daniels was hired as a deputy sheriff. The Danielses were frequently mentioned in newspapers, as they attended various social affairs. In 1889, Daniels was one of the officers held at gunpoint during the infamous Gray County War in Cimarron, Kansas, and escaped unharmed.[83]

Daniels's fellow officers may have liked him, but he eventually wore out his welcome in Bent County. In 1892, the *Rocky Mountain News* reported that he had been drinking with a juggler from a carnival show at the Haymarket Theater in Denver when the conversation turned into a contest of boasts. Daniels's boast was that he was "lightning with a gun." Then he left but soon returned and hit the juggler, Sats Zaroui, over the head with his revolver. When the police arrived, Daniels flashed his badge. Authorities consulted with former lawman Bat Masterson, who knew of Daniels in Dodge City but now ran Denver's Palace Variety Theater. Masterson confirmed that Daniels was no longer a lawman and should not have been wearing a badge at all.[84] With his reputation shot once again, Daniels decided to move to the Cripple Creek District. In May, the *News* revealed, "Ben Daniels, a miner who owns a placer claim in Squaw gulch [*sic*], today washed out two ounces of gold with a common gold pan from his claim. The dirt was not selected for a special test, but was taken from the pay dirt in the gulch, of which he has a large quantity."[85]

Evidence that Daniels still very much enjoyed his sporting lifestyle came two years later, when an ex-deputy named J.R. Wilson was arrested in Denver and brought to Colorado Springs for some "outrage" he allegedly committed there. Wilson told the *Rocky Mountain News* that during the evening he was with "a young lady," the victim of the alleged outrage, until 11:00 p.m. Around that time, Wilson said, he met two men on a downtown corner in Colorado Springs. One of them was Wilson's accuser, a man named Parker. The other man was Daniels. Wilson claimed they played cards until 2:00 a.m. The paper declined to follow up on the charge against Wilson.

Daniels continued mining in the district until 1897, when he managed to infiltrate Cripple Creek's police force. Night Marshal Ed Carberry had been suspended, and Daniels was appointed in his place. Shortly afterward, he became deputy marshal. Just over six months after being appointed, however, Daniels was charged with "malfeasance," the act of wrongdoing by a public official. A hearing was scheduled for December 9.

The charge against Daniels focused on a certain poker table that had been stolen from the cabin of William High. Although High was employed at Johnny Nolon's Saloon in Cripple Creek, nobody seems to have questioned why he had a poker table in his private home. The problem at hand was that during the previous July, High said, the table went missing. He spoke to Marshal Daniels about it, who said it had been found in an abandoned prospect hole by a small boy, who alerted the police. But witness Clabe Jones, who was also on the police force, stated that he knew Daniels had the table, and the two of them had haggled over the price when Jones wanted to buy it—because the item in question wasn't just any poker table. This particular table had two pegs underneath the tabletop. A player sitting at it could use his knee to press one peg to make his unwanted cards mysteriously disappear and the other peg to make his winning cards pop into his hand.

As Daniels went to court, Cripple Creek's rumor mill whispered that his extracurricular activities included working side jobs—like running faro banks in various gambling establishments. Also, Daniels had, at one point, allowed the table in question and a crooked roulette wheel to run at a certain Myers Avenue gambling house in return for payoffs. He also allegedly blackmailed both lawbreakers and even respectable citizens to get his way. No wonder Daniels's trial became a big, confusing mess: Jones testified that Daniels had offered to draw up plans to build a similar cheat table. Nine other witnesses, including mine owner Joe Finley, city jailer Dan Hanley and General Sherman Bell, took the stand but gave several different versions of what they had seen of the crooked table and the gamblers who played at it. Subsequent testimony failed to identify the table as the one used for gambling schemes or even as the one stolen from Mr. High. But even High claimed he had never examined the table closely, and Alonzo Welty, whose family had been around long before there even was a Cripple Creek, withdrew his complaint with the explanation that he had misunderstood the charges.

Once again, Ben Daniels was acquitted of all charges just a week into his trial. But now, far too many people how Daniels had orchestrated bribes and threats, including drunks thrown in the pokey who lined his pockets to secure their release. A Myers Avenue floozy witnessed such clandestine deals while in jail. There were wrongful arrests, and one man was run out of town for "talking too much." A police officer had been fired for interfering in Daniels's business.[86] His antics were too well known in Kansas, Wyoming, Denver, Bent County and now Cripple Creek. What to do?

Daniels's next move was to join Theodore Roosevelt's First United States Volunteer Cavalry, better known as the Rough Riders. Cripple Creek embraced Daniels's decision. "Ben has a record," the *Cripple Creek Morning Times* admitted, describing him "a cold, passionless and secretive man, who goes about his business of thief-catching as relentlessly as a blood hound." The paper also talked about Daniels as a man "who never deserted a friend," was quite handy with a firearm and had "nerves of steel."[87] The honorable act of joining the Rough Riders seems to have automatically redeemed the man from any wrongdoing in Cripple Creek.

Daniels soon left for Texas, where, in no time, he was assigned to the machine group in "K" troop in San Antonio and traveled to Cuba. Cripple Creek's pride for him increased when, amazingly, Daniels was the only member of his company of twenty men to survive a battle. Despite his seedy past, he soon earned accolades for personally serving Roosevelt and even saving the future president's life on San Juan Hill. Even the Cripple Creek Elks Lodge heaped praise on Daniels, calling him "one the best of the Rough Riders remembered by the lodge of which he is a member."[88] The folks of Cripple Creek even stayed in touch with Anna Daniels, who had relocated to Kansas.

In 1898, the *Morning Times* published one of Daniels's letters to Anna. The note described his adventures alongside General Sherman Bell in Cuba in detail, ending with this narcissistic note: "Whoops! What a long

Ben Daniels may be one of the men surrounding Theodore Roosevelt when the Rough Riders were photographed in Cuba during 1898. *Wikimedia Commons.*

letter for me to write. Just make me a leather medal."[89] Even Roosevelt had nothing but good to say about this soldier, showering approval on Daniels's bravery in both Dodge City and during the war. Roosevelt was so proud of Daniels that after the war he appointed him as a U.S. marshal in Arizona, first at Yuma and later Nogales. In addition to his appointment, Daniels also invested in several Arizona mines and was asked by the Papago Natives in Pima County to command a regiment they were forming.

For a short time, Daniels was quite comfortable in his new station. It would be some time before the truth about his past caught up with him, thanks to those who decided to blow the whistle on the con man. "Did Governor Murphy [of Arizona] ever see a game of Faro dealt from behind the table?" sneered the *Durango (CO) Democrat* in 1902.[90] More investigations revealed Daniels's arrest in Montana, as well as his reputation as a onetime "hold-up man." It was none other than Jacob Bloom, whom Daniels had worked for back in Cripple Creek, who revealed the man had committed at least two murders, was a gambler and "dive keeper" and was just plain "an all-around bad man." Although Bloom also declared that Daniels "would do anything for a friend," Arizonans weren't buying the story. Even Roosevelt grew disappointed with his pupil, saying, "You did a grave wrong to me when you failed to be frank…and tell me about this one blot on your record."[91]

In February 1902, Daniels saved Roosevelt further embarrassment by resigning as U.S. marshal. He remained in Arizona, investing in various mines and maintaining his friendship with Roosevelt, who still seemed to feel something for him. Ironically, the most common link between them was that both had been to Cripple Creek. In Roosevelt's case, the first of his two visits there had been less than pleasant. Back in 1900, when Roosevelt was a nominee for vice president of the United States and Daniels was in Cuba, the candidate visited the district on a political mission to convince voters that producing silver coinage would be good for the economy. The people of the district, all of whom relied solely on the gold produced in the district, weren't buying the story.

Several prominent men of the district posed with Roosevelt on his second trip, inside the Portland Mine's Shaft No. 2 in 1901. *Courtesy Victor Lowell Thomas Museum.*

While Finn's Folly looked as fancy as homes came, it quickly fell apart and was dismantled in 1907. *Courtesy Cripple Creek District Museum #2001 163.*

Roosevelt's visit went downhill quickly. He barely survived making a speech at the Victor Armory before an angry mob began edging too close. His bodyguards, along with postmaster Danny Sullivan, struggled to keep the crowd at bay, got Roosevelt back on the train and quickly made for Cripple Creek, where things went a lot smoother. Impressed by the scenery and gracious treatment by his hosts, Roosevelt promised to visit the district again in a few months. J. Maurice Finn, the prominent attorney who would later represent the alleged train robber Bob Lee, managed to accompany Roosevelt on his tour of the town and offered to put him up on his next visit. Roosevelt accepted.

After he was elected vice president in 1901, Roosevelt kept his word and planned a second visit to the district. The trouble for Finn was, his little house on Irene Street that was hardly fit for a vice president of the United States. The attorney quickly borrowed a considerable sum of money from Colorado Trading and Transfer Company owner A.E. Carlton to erect a palatial mansion in which to lodge Roosevelt. The home that emerged was a grand mess of turrets, a widow's walk, spacious porches and five floors of exquisite furniture with an indoor fountain, plus electricity throughout. Finn called it the Towers.

True to his word, Roosevelt returned in August, just a month before being appointed president following the death of President William McKinley. Unfortunately for Finn, Roosevelt came to the district via the Colorado Springs and Cripple Creek District Railroad, which dropped him off in Victor first. He was royally received by an apologetic populace, and they say he shook the hand of every resident of Victor as they lined the streets. He also was treated to a tour of the Porland Mine.

By the time Roosevelt boarded the train for Cripple Creek, time constraints did not allow him to get any farther than the front porch of the Towers. He did admire the staff Finn had hired and called the place "the most beautiful home in Colorado." Then he left, leaving the robust little Finn standing there much like a deflated balloon. The residents of Cripple Creek could not help but snicker. Folks began calling the Towers "Finn's Folly." Finn himself called it a "monument to a damned fool."[92] Whether he meant himself or Roosevelt was never clarified.

If Roosevelt's second trip to the district taught him one thing, it was that a friend, or supporter, could turn on you at the drop of a dime. So when Daniels hit him up for a job in 1904, Roosevelt responded positively by hiring his friend as the superintendent at Arizona's notorious prison in Yuma. He was still there when his first wife, Anna, died in 1906 and when he married Anna Evaline Stakebake in 1908. A year later, after Roosevelt left office, Daniels was asked to resign his position and offered a job as an "Indian agent" in Wisconsin. He declined the offer, preferring to remain in Arizona. From then on, his name only occasionally popped up in newspapers. In 1917, it was noted that he had presented his old friend Roosevelt with a "handsome cane beautifully fashioned from cow horns by a convict in the Arizona prison."[93] Daniels also ran for sheriff of Pima County twice and lost but finally won on his third try in 1920. Three years later, Daniels died in Tucson. Anna followed in 1946. Today, Ben Daniels's antics in Cripple Creek are remembered as one of the highlights in the life of the loyal problem child of Teddy Roosevelt's Rough Riders.

THE VIXEN WHO BURNED DOWN VICTOR

*L*ike any growing frontier town, the city of Victor, founded in 1891, soon had its share of wanton women. Within five years, Victor became the Cripple Creek District's second-largest city. In the wake of Cripple Creek's infamous fires, the 1896 Cripple Creek District Directory for Victor noted proudly that the city's fire department "is especially efficient, being offered by men of long experience in eastern cities....The Victor Water Works adds greatly to the comforts and wants of her citizens." Despite this comforting fact, however, Victor was as vulnerable to fire as any western mining town. Due to the many mines around the city, Victor was considered a blue-collar town, since many miners lived there. Alternatively, Cripple Creek was known as the city where the wealthier populace lived, but the two cities did have many similarities. Both were served by railroads, businesses, churches and schools. Like Cripple Creek, Victor had at least one opera house and a generous handful of theaters. The most ironic commonality is that both Victor and Cripple Creek suffered disastrous fires during the late 1890s, and each one was started by a woman in the red-light district.

By the mid-1890s, there were numerous drinking houses along Victor Avenue. Many more were located on South Third Street between Victor and Portland Avenues. Among the businesses on South Third was the Albany Hotel, which included a tavern and rented rooms to miners. Saloons included those owned by Henry Bahne, Daniel Hanley, George Rodgers, Charlie Seitz, Rufus R. Stoddard, Victor Weisburg and Nelson

Johnson's "Victor Garden," as well as the Combination Saloon and Billiard Hall, Sexton and Burris and Whalen and Neville. Another entertainment was the Theatre Comique, located close to Portland Avenue and identified as a "dive" on the Sanborn Fire Insurance Map. Although many "boardinghouses" were on South Third, it was commonly known that some of them were brothels—especially along "Paradise Alley," the thoroughfare west of the Theatre Comique between Third and Fourth Streets. Not surprisingly, several single women were identified in the 1896 Cripple Creek District Directory as living in the neighborhood with no occupation listed for them. Those women who were gainfully employed included Belle Felch and Anna Johnson, who each ran a lodging house. Hannah Gonsalves and Anna Lee made ladies' hats. Jennie Grant and Grace Masher were dressmakers. Jessie Kittredge offered laundry services. Other businesses included a barber, a cigar and tobacco shop, two grocery stores, a meat market, two restaurants and no fewer than five tailors.

WOMEN WITH NO OCCUPATION ON SOUTH THIRD STREET, 1896
(between Victor and Portland Avenues)

Mary C. Boswell
Minerva Brannen
Laura E. Coake
Mamie Dedrick
Hattie Dixson
Carrie Elston
Florence Gains
Florence Jennings
Nellie Kirk
Nancy Martin
Ella McNann
Rachel E. Moser
Margaret Muckenthaler
Elizabeth Phillips
Mary Reilly
Louise Reitenbach
Florence Rogers
Maude Spencer

Four other occupants of South Third Street bear mention. The singing Togerson Sisters, May and Anna, along with national performers Lottie and Polly Oatley, kept their own quarters on South Third. The 1896 directory identifies the Oatley girls as performing at the Union Theater, also located on South Third. The sisters would eventually move on to other venues across the west, including the Regina Saloon in Dawson City, Alaska. The girls had a small dog named Tiny that would sing along with them in a soprano voice. South Third Street was one busy place indeed.

One of the most notorious dance halls on South Third Street was the Turf Saloon. The bar may have been in the building identified on the 1896 Sanborn map as the Theatre Comique, the only place on South

Part of Victor's red-light district at Portland and South Third Streets is visible behind the Eclipse Livery Stables, 1894. *Courtesy Victor Lowell Thomas Museum.*

Third that appears large enough to house several occupants and had a stage. William Claude Monroe is identified as the proprietor of the dance hall. Max Clements, John D. Ready, Henry Warner and Henry Williams were employed as bartenders. David Bales was a dance "caller," and Joseph Darrin worked as an actor. Bales and Clements's wives, Ethel and Louise, also lived on the premises. Seven other women—Rosa Buchfink, Minnie Davenport, Jennie Fryberger, Pauline Pease, Minnie and Margaret Williams and Jennie Young—also lived and worked at the Turf. Although there is no doubt that the ladies of the Turf Saloon made their way by dancing with customers for money, they likely offered much more.

The Turf Saloon was certainly not alone in offering entertainment and liquor to male patrons. Throughout 1897, the *Victor Record* advertised and wrote about various watering holes along South Third Street, who owned them and who was staging the latest grand opening. Paradise Alley merited plenty of mention as well: in January, a man named Gannon, alias Fait, was arrested for cohabitating with a Black woman with the last name of

Bumgardner. That same month, two other Black women went to court after fighting over a mutual fiancé. When a young man parted ways with a cyprian in March, she got even with him by stealing his clothes. In April, Mollie Patton was fined for raising a ruckus in the alley. In August, two men were caught fighting over a "Paradise Alley damsel" near Portland Avenue. And in January 1898, it was noted that the cribs and primitive brothels along Portland Avenue were growing out of control.

Victorites took the stories of such antics in stride, but one article in particular during 1898 was a real attention-grabber. The story concerned Nellie Taylor, the wife of Bob Taylor, who had robbed the Florence and Cripple Creek Railroad in 1895 and was still lingering in prison. Nellie lived at the Turf Saloon. On March 11, the *Victor Record* reported a most distressing story concerning Eva Taylor, Nellie's sixteen-year-old daughter. For some time, Eva had been begging for help because Nellie's paramour, a Goldfield saloon owner named L.S. Moore, had been brutally raping the girl for a whole year—with Nellie's assistance.

The people of Goldfield and Victor were no strangers to Eva's story. For some months prior, the Victor Woman's Club had tried to take the girl to a good home in Kansas. Unfortunately, it was up to Nellie to release her daughter into their custody, and at the last minute she changed her mind. Even as authorities worked to put Moore behind bars, the seasoned criminal was in Goldfield making threats against anyone willing to testify against him. He was deposited in the jail at Cripple Creek anyway, while Nellie was taken to the Victor jail. After the preliminary hearing a week later, the pair were taken to Colorado Springs. In May, Nellie was released. A month after that, Moore was sentenced to sixteen years in prison. What happened to Eva and Nellie Taylor in the wake of Moore's conviction? Nobody knew, and the truth was that the bawdy women of South Third Street came and went so frequently that it was hard to keep track of them, save for the occasional article.

Shortly after Nellie Taylor was freed, the *Record* turned its attention to the attempted suicide of Fannie Smith, who also worked at the Turf Saloon. This time, the newspaper decided to report the incident in the same unsympathetic humor as so many other newspapers in the American West:

About 5 o'clock yesterday morning the lodgers over the Turf saloon on South 3rd street were awakened by a sensational episode in the room occupied by Fannie Smith, a dance hall girl. Fannie had some trouble with her lover, and just to show that she was a good girl she swallowed a vial of laudanum in the presence of her friends. After the farewells had all been said and Fannie began to hear the golden harps Dr. Boyd arrived with a stomach pump and removed the laudanum, which was a little worse for wear but still good enough for suicidal purposes. Last night Fannie was still in bed but the physician says she will be able to make it all up with her recreant lover and live until the next time.[94]

The *Record* continued reporting on the drunken antics, parties, fights and general mayhem in Paradise Alley and along South Third Street and Portland Avenue. One article, published on July 29, 1899, is especially interesting: Some lucky young boy was given a miniature replica of a hook and ladder fire wagon. The child became infatuated with all things firefighting. Recently, he had been duly impressed by the extinguishing of a fake "conflagration" being demonstrated at a local carnival. During the Fourth of July, he had also watched in fascination as the local firemen had participated in a "hose laying contest." A few days after the carnival, the boy and his friends were playing with his fire wagon in Paradise Alley when they decided to construct a replica model of the hose house at the Victor Fire Department itself.

The replica, said the *Record*, "had the box stalls, the drop harness [for hooking up horses] and even the door chain of the original." The owner of the fire wagon had great fun pulling it around as his friends cheered him on. When the novelty ran out, the group decided to go further with the game—by piling some old newspapers on a dilapidated shed, setting fire to it and alerting the fire station so they could watch the action. Fortunately, two firemen immediately dashed down the alley with the real hook and ladder truck and doused the flames quickly. The *Record* noted that in the aftermath it was "strange enough the owners of the buildings along Paradise Alley objected to the realism of this game and sat down on it so hard that the boys were compelled to invent some other form of diversion."[95] What nobody could know was that less than a month later, another fire would break out in Paradise Alley and prove every bit destructive as the one in Cripple Creek three years before.

On the afternoon of Monday, August 21, the ladies of Paradise Alley were regrouping after partying away the weekend. Among them was a French woman, Jennie Thompson.[96] Her place, a small shack, was near the 999 Dance Hall, located near Portland Avenue. Some say Jennie owned the place. Others identified the joint as being, or at least offering, an opium den.

Unfortunately, however, information about the woman, where she came from or how long she had been in Victor is scant.

According to the *Record*, one of Jennie's garments had a stain on it. The best way to get it out was to clean it with gasoline. At the time, gas was commonly used to clean clothing stains, even by respectable folks. The trouble was, although Jennie had thought to step outside into the fresh air to clean the garment, she was smoking a cigarette as she did so. Another woman saw what she was doing and warned her of how dangerous it was, to which Jennie "made a contemptuous reply." Exactly what she said was lost to the wind as the cigarette fell from her lips. It landed near enough to the small pan of gas that the fumes ignited a fire.[97]

Within seconds, flames seemed to be licking everything—Jennie's garment, Jennie's shack and maybe even Jennie herself. Three boys in the area witnessed what happened and ran toward the fire station hollering "Fire!" In the meantime, smoke was curling between Jennie's cabin and the 999 as flames began crawling up the walls of both buildings. Although it took firemen only four minutes to hook up the horses and get the fire wagon to the scene, there was some sort of trouble with turning on the water. Within five minutes, the flames had reached the roof of Jennie's place as the wind fanned it into an inferno. No amount of water was going to put it out.

Great plumes of smoke rise above Victor as the fire makes its way up South Third Street. *Courtesy Cripple Creek District Museum.*

It was literally only minutes before the fire grew enough to jump across South Third Street to the Dewey Dance Hall, two groceries owned by Beach and Ketelsen and the numerous saloons on the east side of the street. One by one they all caught fire as the conflagration worked its way toward Victor Avenue, burning buildings on both sides of the street as it went. There was nothing anyone could do at that point but grab what they could and get out of the fire's path. The flames soon reached the business section of town. Gone were J.B. Cunningham's lumberyard, the Monarch Saloon, several markets and shops, the Hotel Victor and the Gold Coin Mine, among dozens of other buildings. Even the Midland Terminal Depot north of downtown was lost.

For hours, folks piled goods into the streets to save them, only to watch them burn. Others were able to throw items into express wagons and get them to the city limits, where others anxiously awaited their families. Still others could only stare in shock as the entire downtown burned to the ground—twelve blocks in all. Some lost everything they had. "I have the wife and children left," lamented one man, "and that is all I had to begin with."[98] Then came the looters who daringly pulled bottles of liquor from the burning buildings and began imbibing freely. As night fell, the National Guard was called in to arrest any remaining thieves as residents picked

Like Cripple Creek, the city of Victor quickly built itself back up to a first-class metropolis. *Courtesy Victor Lowell Thomas Museum.*

through the smoking rubble looking for their belongings and hundreds of small fires continued burning under the rising moon. Thankfully, nobody had been killed.

In the coming days, supplies and food were given out at Washington School and other places to those in need. Those business owners who still had some merchandise set up shop in other parts of town or over in Goldfield. As Victor put its city back together, citizens realized that, like Cripple Creek in 1896, now was the perfect time to rebuild a bigger and better city with fine brick buildings. Within a week or two, a host of optimistic articles in the *Record* talked about the rebuilding as if it were indeed Phoenix rising from the ashes.

What about Jennie Thompson, the woman accused of starting the great fire of Victor? She does not appear to have been held accountable, perhaps because her blunder truly was a mistake. Or maybe she managed to skedaddle out of town before accusing eyes could turn on her. Besides, the city soon realized that the fire signaled the end of bawdy South Third Street, Portland Avenue and Paradise Alley. "With the disappearance of the cribs and their inmates Portland should become one of the desirable business streets of the city," the *Record* crowed.[99] The newspaper clearly underestimated Victor's wanton women; within a short time, the red-light district would make a reprise on Second Street in the locale of today's Victor Bowl of Gold ballpark.

JOE MOORE AND A
DEADLY PARADE

*E*verybody liked Joe Moore. The musician/bartender/host extraordinaire had been around Cripple Creek since 1894 and was well known for his band and membership in the District Musician's Union. If there was a party, there was Moore, usually serving up libations from behind the bar or serving as toastmaster at the local Bohemian Club. "If you can catch Joe Moore, the genial mixologist at Becker & Nolon's, in a communicative mood he can give you some experiences that will make your hair stand on end," teased the local papers.[100] Yes, everybody like Joe Moore—except one man, Jim McVicar. And nobody would know just how much McVicar hated Moore until one fateful day in March 1899.

When the gold boom first began in the Cripple Creek District, the entire area was part of El Paso County. That meant that mining claims and official government business had to be conducted in far-away Colorado Springs, the county seat. But the real trouble was, much of the revenues from the district in the way of taxes, business licenses and assorted fees all went to the county offices. Very little of it returned to the city governments in the district. As early as 1892, local citizens had complained and suggested that perhaps it would be better to form a new county. El Paso County commissioner J.C. Plumb initially agreed, but once the gold values in the district were truly realized, he and his fellow commissioners changed their minds. A new county would mean lost revenue for El Paso County.

Undaunted, the wealthy mining men of the district garnered enough support in 1897 to propose forming a new county, Sylvanite. The bill was

Becker & Nolon's, aka Johnny Nolon's Casino, still looks just like it did when Joe Moore served up libations there. *Author's collection.*

of course shot down by the senate when voting time came around. For two more years, city governments around the district continued pushing to create their own county. They also chose a new name: Teller County, in honor of Senator Henry M. Teller, who had been serving Colorado off and on since 1876.

Over the next two years, officials throughout the district continued to rally for the new county. As election time drew near in early 1899, the opposition from Colorado Springs remained quite strong. There was even some dissention in Cripple Creek, going by newspaper accounts of heated debates and bar fights over the matter. Come election day, however, Teller County won. The new county was formed from parts of western El Paso County and northern Fremont County. Colorado governor C.S. Thomas was slated to sign the measure on March 13, 1899, right there in Cripple Creek.

News about the election came on Thursday, and Thomas would be signing the paperwork on Monday. Accordingly, Cripple Creek mayor

Charles Pierce declared an extended weekend holiday. Schools and most businesses closed, but the saloons remained open as a grand parade was planned down Bennett Avenue. Police chief McDaniel would ride a stunning black horse at the front. Mayor Pierce and Governor Thomas would follow in a beautiful coach. The fire department, six marching bands, two drum corps, thirty-four fraternal lodges from around the district and numerous floats were lined up to toss Pear's Soap, Malt Nutrine, Pozzoni's Face Powder and other party favors to parade watchers. And as a member of the Cripple Creek Elks Lodge, Joe Moore was to lead the parade wearing a jaunty purple uniform with brass buttons and gold fringe.

CRIPPLE CREEK WENT WILD

Passage of Teller County Bill Creates Great Enthusiasm.

All the Towns in the District Join in the Rejoicing When the Measure Finally Shoots the Legislative Rapids Formal Celebration Will be Held.

The *Grand Junction Daily Sentinel* accurately described the excitement when Teller County was formed. *Public domain.*

What few people knew was that the previous week, Moore had a falling out with a blacksmith named William Tobey. Around the same time, Moore had thrown a drunk, Jim McVicar, out of Tom Lorimer's saloon. Tobey and McVicar were now drinking together and seethed as they watched Moore joyfully leading the parade down Bennett Avenue. Everyone was having so much fun that the band kept playing as Moore turned around and led them back up Bennett Avenue. Dozens of people joyfully followed the parade as it wove its way back and forth across Bennett Avenue in a serpentine fashion.

As the group neared Lorimer's saloon, McVicar and Tobey appeared outside and accosted Moore. Heated words were exchanged before Moore suddenly drew his revolver and hit Tobey over the head several times. McVicar shouted, "Don't kill that man!" as he pulled Tobey away. The twosome threw Moore to the ground, wrenching the revolver from the prostrate man and hitting him on the head with it. Moore and Tobey were still wrestling on the sidewalk when McVicar leaned in and shot Joe Moore clean through the head. He was carried into the saloon, where he died within twenty minutes.[101]

Tobey and McVicar were taken to the city jail as people began talking about what a good guy Joe Moore had been. He had only recently married and was just thirty-five years old. Like McVicar, Moore had been in the district for many years. Most of those who knew McVicar claimed he was usually a "steady and temperate young man."[102] But Moore's murder changed the way people thought about McVicar for sure. Tobey was soon out of jail, but McVicar stayed behind bars awaiting his fate and refusing to talk about the incident.

Joe Moore's funeral on March 11 was one of the largest Cripple Creek would ever see. The Elks Lodge gave him the grandest funeral they could muster, and the *Cripple Creek Morning Times* published a heartfelt poem to the man:

> *Farewell, Joe Moore, we wish you well in that mysterious land to which you go;*
> *We loved you well, and knew you as you were—A staunch and trusty friend in weal or woe.*
> *Farewell, Joe Moore, we'll meet you presently, In that great lodge room over in the skies,*
> *Where, once again, with warm, fraternal clasp You'll welcome us within that paradise.*
> *Farewell, Joe Moore, we grieve to see you go, And leave us here upon this earthly shore;*
> *We hope and know that we shall meet again In that bright land where parting comes no more.*[103]

Every business in town closed for one hour during Moore's service. The lodge was "packed to overflowing and hundreds were forced to remain on the outside" reported the *Morning Times*. Moore's casket could barely be seen under the mound of flowers, including a bouquet from his new wife, the former Jennie Taylor, that included a note which "carried a little secret that only two hearts ever knew, and one has ceased to beat." After the services, Moore's casket was slowly carried through the crowd, which included members of the Red Men and the Western Federation of Miners. At the Midland Terminal Depot, the coffin was loaded onto a train and shipped off to Denver. The *Morning Times* would tell how "the music was not good. Notes were missed now and then when a friend thought of some kindly act of the departed."[104]

In the days following the funeral, all eyes turned to local newspapers to see what would happen to McVicar. He pleaded not guilty on March 14 and was able to bond out for $5,000. He also noticed that the public in

It would be 1905 before the newly constructed Teller County Courthouse would be dedicated. *Courtesy Cripple Creek District Museum.*

general was less than friendly—a lot less. He tried requesting a change of venue for his trial, but it was for naught. The public was ready to convict McVicar, and even that "hot-shot lawyer, J. Maurice Finn, stepped in on behalf of Joe Moore," noted the *Victor Daily Record*. In court, McVicar's attorneys, Crowell and Lombard of Colorado Springs, tried to portray Moore as a "brutal man." Nobody was buying their story for a second.[105]

For the next two days, a dozen jury members listened as McVicar and Tobey were grilled, and witnesses testified about what they heard and saw. The trouble was, not everybody saw the same thing. Some said McVicar shot Moore in the head, but others believed the gun went off while the men struggled on the sidewalk. In the end, after a long afternoon of deliberating, the jury voted across the board to acquit McVicar. The case was closed, McVicar disappeared from Cripple Creek forever and residents of the district got back to business. After all, there was an all-new county to tend to.

TO TEASE A DYING MAN

*N*o matter where the Cripple Creek District's residents came from, the effects of living at high altitude in primitive conditions could make anyone into a brutish scalawag under the right circumstances. Although there were thousands of upper-class citizens in the district, an equal number of miners who had been optimistic in their search for gold were met with hard times and harsh living conditions instead. For many of them, their failure to find riches bound them to stay, unable to afford to leave in search of greener pastures. It was, in several ways, a vicious cycle. By 1901, poor living and hard drinking had transformed many of these men into harsh, hardened dregs of society. And nothing better illustrates the gritty, lowdown roughnecks of Cripple Creek than the story of James "Silver" Roberts.

Roberts was just one of thousands of miners who toiled in the mines daily. He was likely the same man who appeared in San Miguel County census during 1885: both were born in 1850 in Wales and immigrated to America in 1873. How and when he got to Cripple Creek is unknown, and his only relative, brother John, lived in Elkton. Very little else was known about the man, including which mine he worked in. And it is just a guess that James Roberts was accustomed to spending at least some of his leisure time at the Dawson Club in the bawdy district of Myers Avenue.

The Dawson Club at 317 Myers Avenue had great hopes when it first opened in January 1900 as a vaudeville theater. The first—and perhaps only—professional performance there was Billy McCall and the King

Sisters, who played a four-week engagement. As of January 30, 1901, proprietor William Brooks was openly advertising in Denver's *Rocky Mountain News* for "ladies who are good singers."[106] And six months later, the *News* also reported that Harry A. Couch, lately of Denver, and William Stillman, the pianist at the Dawson Club, had been arrested for forgery. Couch was arrested in Pueblo as Stillman was apprehended in Cripple Creek.

Given that the Dawson Club was in the heart of Cripple Creek's red-light district, it is not surprising that the place quickly devolved into just another local dive. On Christmas night in 1901, Roberts came into the place with some friends to imbibe in a little Christmas cheer. Notably, the man was normally "an inoffensive, quiet man when not in his cups."[107] But in his cups Roberts unfortunately was when his friends bid him a Merry Christmas sometime after midnight and left the bar. That's when the trouble began.

Various newspapers reported different versions of the story. According to the *Leadville Herald Democrat*, Roberts soon got into a scuffle with several men: Brooks, Jack Varley, W.J. Fletcher, "Doc" Howell, Edward J. McCarten and someone named Mullins, as well as a woman identified as Lily Arlington. Alternatively, the *Rocky Mountain News* listed the names

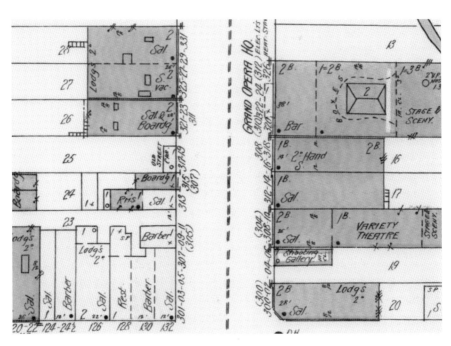

The Dawson Club replaced a former trolley car, which can be seen occupying lot 25 on this 1900 Sanborn Fire Insurance Map. *Library of Congress.*

of those involved as Jack Whiting, Jack Crowley, Ed McCarten and C.C. Howell. Whoever really was present, Roberts and Whiting were soon engaged in a "wordy quarrel."[108] Roberts pulled a knife and was knocked down. He regained his footing and next went after Crowley but was tackled and forced down on the floor. Then Brooks stepped from behind the bar with a .45-caliber Colt pistol. Brooks would later claim that Roberts stood up and "slashed at him with his knife."[109] When he failed to hit his mark, Roberts spewed some epithets and threats as he turned toward the door. He never reached it. Instead, he was struck from behind on the right side of his head. As he fell, Roberts hit his head on the wood-burning stove and again when he hit the floor.

The *Herald Democrat* claimed that Mullins had stepped in to break up a fight after Roberts "slashed" the man identified as Varley a few times with a knife, and it was Varley who threw Roberts to the floor. The paper also verified that Roberts suffered two skull fractures. Also, Brooks "grabbed

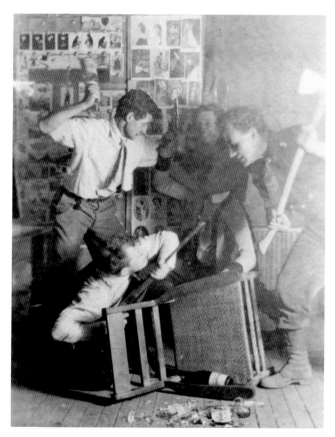

A staged barroom fight in the Cripple Creek District, date unknown, gives an idea of what happened at the Dawson Club. *Courtesy Cripple Creek District Museum.*

a gun to stop the quarrel, and says in his excitement he may have struck Roberts and killed him."[110] Brooks maintained that he used his gun only as a means to stop the fight. But it was not so much that Brooks whacked Roberts on the head as he tried to leave, nor that Roberts hit his head twice more as he crumpled to the floor. It was what happened in the time after the man was down.

All witnesses in the bar agreed that there was no question that James Roberts was severely injured. Blood was flowing freely from his head as he lay on the floor, and he made no effort to get up. Yet the drunken crowd jeered at him anyway, calling him names. When Roberts didn't respond, he was eventually dragged to the back of the room, and someone threw a glass of water in his face to revive him. "Come on up here, Slim, and have a drink, you —— —— ——," jeered one of the men.[111] The teasing went on for about an hour before talk began of throwing the unconscious Roberts into the alley.

Around 4:00 a.m., it was finally decided that a doctor should be summoned. The most reliable source in this story identifies the physician as Dr. J.W. Sanders, who soon found out why Roberts could not get up: he had died from his injuries right there in the Dawson Club. Police were called and arrested six of the witnesses until their stories could be sorted out. Roberts's body was taken to Sanders's office as Coroner T.J. Dunn came over from Victor. Two days later, Dunn's findings were revealed by the coroner's jury: "We, the Jury, find the deceased, James Roberts, came to his death in the Dawson club [sic] by a blow from some blunt instrument held in the hands of William Brooks."[112] A preliminary hearing was set for the following day. It is notable that three of the witnesses—Whiting, McCartin and Crowley—were former policemen. Equally notable is that John Roberts was named as the prosecuting witness.

Brooks quickly cast about for the best lawyer he could find. And find he did, engaging the illustrious lawyer J. Maurice Finn to represent him. Finn had made the news on at least two occasions in the preceding year alone. The first time was in May 1900, when he defended Hole in the Wall gang member Bob Lee, who was found guilty and sent to prison. The second time happened a few months later when Finn foolishly spent thousands building a fancy house to impress Vice President Theodore Roosevelt.

Despite Finn's very public failures, Brooks trusted that the lawyer, who was fondly nicknamed the "Oratorical Whirlwind of the West," would get him off. Finn's evidence gathering included an extended examination of Roberts's corpse before it was buried in an unmarked grave at Cripple

Creek's Mt. Pisgah Cemetery. On March 6, 1902, Finn, along with fellow attorney S.D. Crump, filed into the courthouse for Brooks's trial along with Prosecuting Attorney Henry Trowbridge, Deputy District Attorney Cole, a man named John Glover and several witnesses. In his opening statements, Finn announced that Roberts, a poor immigrant, was malnourished as a child. That, he said, was why Brooks's pistol was able to put such a dent in Roberts's abnormally thin cranium. When Finn suddenly reached into his valise and pulled out an actual piece of Roberts's gruesome skull as evidence, those in the courtroom were aghast.

Parading the skull around the courtroom like the king's crown, Finn made sure to point out the cracks at the point of contact. Witnesses would testify how on the night of his death, Roberts had busted up the furniture in the Dawson Club and brandished his deadly little pocketknife. Three days later, the jury, after deliberation lasting thirty-eight hours, found Brooks not guilty of manslaughter. The *Rocky Mountain News* would report that "Brooks took the decision evidently in a calm way, but his brother, Fred Brooks of Denver, broke down and cried like a child." Later that night, Brooks announced he "would leave Cripple Creek for good and in all probability would go to California."[113]

Brooks's announcement was probably just as well, since one article claimed the man was "nearly mobbed by those who liked Roberts, and got out of town on the next train."[114] The piece was written by Jack Bell, a former miner who went to work as a newspaper reporter in 1902. Bell didn't write about the affair until 1904, when he was working for the *Denver Post* and favored writing good investigative stories. It was he who revealed that a party of twenty-five deputies accompanied Brooks to the Midland Terminal Depot to ensure he got on the next train out of town safely. Brooks never returned to Cripple Creek, opting to live out his life in Seattle, Washington. What really intrigued Bell was the part about Finn procuring the piece of Roberts's skull that won Brooks's freedom. And his story was about as colorful as they come.

Bell's article detailed how Finn assisted the mortician who removed the piece of skull from Roberts's head. When Finn got there, the top of the cranium had already been removed, and he saw the skin of Roberts's scalp flopped over the victim's face. "Here, Finn," the mortician said to the attorney, "help me fix up this scalp in a decent way so the head will look natural." Finn offered up a wad of newspaper. "That won't do," the coroner said, "it will absorb the moisture and the scalp will settle and look bad. Find something, quick, somebody will drop in here in a minute and there would be something unpleasant happen."[115] When Finn found a dirty towel lying nearby, the mortician approved. Together, the men, their hands and arms covered with Roberts's blood, tucked the towel into the corpse's skull and sewed the scalp together.

Over time, the story of James Roberts was forgotten. The grim piece of evidence was stored alongside items from other cases in the Teller County Courthouse, where it sat undisturbed for just over seventy years. Most ironically, in 1973, the State of Colorado ruled that weak bones and thin skulls were no longer valid excuses for cases dealing in bodily harm by another resulting in death. It was around this same time that attorney P.J. Anderson, who worked at the Teller County Courthouse, happened to run across the partial skull of James Roberts. The evidence was sitting next to a small bag of gold dust from another trial long ago.

When Anderson talked of his find, word spread like wildfire through the district. Believing the two pieces of evidence were linked, a handful of folks claimed some sort of kinship to Roberts. In the end, however, the gold dust was only worth some eighteen dollars and had nothing to do with Roberts, and the claims quickly faded. Still, Anderson was interested in the history of the skull and performed his own research until he found the original story. Someone else was interested in the skull as well: restaurateur Dave Lux, who owned Concept Restaurants in Colorado Springs. The company specialized in themed eateries, and one of them was a steakhouse named for J. Maurice Finn. But although Lux offered to take the skull, Anderson later verified, the presiding judge declined because he wanted to use it himself—as a novelty ashtray.

The top of James Roberts's skull remains on display at the Cripple Creek District Museum. *Author's collection.*

Fortunately, the ashtray idea never came to fruition. Roberts's skull piece remained in the evidence room of the courthouse. "It was somewhere on the floor, in the corner out of everyone's way," Anderson remembered.[116] Later, it was put on display for a time. It seemed that nobody knew just what to do with it, until 2009. That is when Anderson happened to advertise a television for sale on Craigslist, and an employee of the Teller County Courthouse answered the ad. Anderson told the employee the story of the skull, and she relayed the story to her co-workers, including court reporter Lisa Wheatcraft. Thankfully, Wheatcraft knew all about James Roberts and his skull piece.

What happened next was more fortuitous than anyone could know. Wheatcraft decided to contact the Cripple Creek District Museum and see if there was any interest in adding the skull to their artifact collection. The museum agreed, but Wheatcraft soon discovered that the skull was missing. After making inquiries, she was able to find the historic item again: a former courthouse employee had taken it home with her to keep the skull from becoming the victim of another joke or worse. The section of skull was returned and is today on display at the museum. Plans at the time were to reunite the artifact with Roberts's body, if his burial site could ever be located. Unfortunately, however, thousands of burial records were lost in the tragic burning of the Weiner Block on Bennett Avenue in 1940. Thus, the location of James Roberts's grave may never be known.

THE PLIGHT OF PYROMANIAC ROY BOURQUIN

*I*n Cripple Creek, he was called such unkind nicknames as "Armless," "Armie" and even "Hook." By today's standards, he might have been institutionalized, or perhaps treated with drugs to keep him from the impulses he had no control over. During the 1890s, however, pyromania—a mental disorder that creates a type of stress that can be relieved only by setting fires—was largely misunderstood. So was young Roy Bourquin, living in his own private, fiery hell in a world that had no idea how to help him. Worse yet, few even offered to.

Bourquin's family background gives scant clues as to the cause of his affliction. His parents, Adolphus and Matilda, already had three children—Molly, Jennie and Lulu—by the time they were identified in Ohio during the 1870 census. Ten years later, Adolphus had remarried to another woman, Hannah (née Boleyn). A fourth child, Charles, was born in Washington, Kansas. It would be seven years before Roy, the last of the Bourquin children, was born on April 2, 1887.

Notable is that just a month before Roy's birth, the *Washington Weekly Post* commented that Hannah, "formerly a resident of Washington but now a resident of Greenleaf," was spending time with friends.[117] Whether the Bourquin marriage was on the rocks is up for debate, but the family seemed destined for trouble. Hannah died in about 1889. Two years later, Adolphus filed a claim for injuries he incurred during his Civil War service. When the family moved to Colorado in about 1894, only Adolphus and son Charles came west. Roy, who perhaps was already exhibiting symptoms of his illness, had been left behind with his aunt Susan Bolin in Woodbury, Kansas.[118]

The first news item about Roy in Colorado was when the *Washington Republican* in Kansas reported that after living with his aunt for several years, the boy had been reunited with his father in Cripple Creek. That was in June 1894, and it was soon apparent that something was wrong with the child. Experts today theorize that mental illness like Bourquin's could have been caused by some sort of abuse or neglect, or some other traumatic experience, perhaps even the death of his mother. Alternatively, the child's brain structure or chemistry might have been the culprit. Either way, young Bourquin was alarmingly infatuated with setting fires and other unhealthy impulses.

In 1900, Bourquin had his first brush with the law. That May, the *Victor Record* reported that the teen had been charged with petty larceny. There surely had been more than one violation committed, however, because Bourquin was sentenced to the Colorado State Industrial School in Golden. The school opened in 1881 as "a humane and progressive rehabilitative school for incorrigible young men between the ages of 7 and 16."[119] By the time the 1900 census was taken, the eleven-year-old (the *Record* mistakenly reported Bourquin as being fifteen years old) was enrolled at the school.[120] Sloppy school records mistakenly stated he was born in 1889, and his parents were simply recorded as being born in America. Bourquin's father and brother, meanwhile, lived in Gold Hill Gulch just outside of Cripple Creek.

Bourquin did not remain at the industrial school for long. By 1902, he was back in Cripple Creek when a most tragic incident occurred. On June 16, the *Rocky Mountain News* reported on what happened:

> *One of the most deplorable accidents that ever happened in Cripple Creek occurred in Poverty Gulch about 7:30 o'clock tonight. While playing with powder, Roy Bourquin, aged 14 years and the son of Adolph Bourquin, had both hands blown off. His scalp was badly injured as well as having his entire body peppered full of holes. The Bourquin boy, with George and John Anderson, boys of his own age, got hold of the powder. They adjusted a cap and a fuse to it and dug a hole in the soft dirt and then ignited the fuse. The injured boy was engaged in piling loose dirt with both hands on the powder when it exploded. His right hand was taken off just above the wrist and the left was blown off halfway to the elbow. He was taken to the [St. Nicholas Hospital] where an operation was performed that probably*

will result in his death. It is the belief of the doctors in attendance that one or both of his eyes are blown out also. The playmates of young Bourquin escaped without a scratch.[121]

Bourquin survived. He lost sight in one eye, but the loss of his hands put him forever at the mercy of the state and others, especially after Adolphus Bourquin died in December 1904. In May 1905, the *Rocky Mountain News* reported that Bourquin was in Denver, where he was brought to the police station. The boy explained that he and his brother were sent to live with a Mrs. Will White, who was paid twenty-five dollars a month by the county for their care. Mrs. White had brought the children to Denver. "Since then," Bourquin told the paper, "she has been mistreating me in every way, so I just couldn't stay with her." The brothers were living at a boardinghouse while the local Humane Society (which back then focused on people in need rather than animals) figured out what to do with them. According to Bourquin's statement, he had already been turned away by the public school system due to his disabilities and had also been deemed a "nuisance."[122]

What happened to Charles Bourquin was never mentioned. And whatever efforts were made on behalf of Roy Bourquin in Denver, they were for naught. Authorities tried to send him back to Cripple Creek to live at the Teller County Hospital and Poor House, but he would routinely return to Denver. In 1905, it was reported that he had partnered with an unidentified man described as being around thirty years old and partially blind. Bourquin's job was to walk door to door begging for food and money, which he would give to the man. More recently, a kindly nurse from the Humane Society had personally accompanied Bourquin to the train so he could return to Cripple Creek once more. But "traveling around in company with a companion seems to be more agreeable to the boy than living at the expense of the county at home," the *Rocky Mountain News* commented, "and he returns to Denver at every opportunity he gets."[123]

Bourquin did eventually return to Cripple Creek, where he continued living at the Teller County Hospital. But by 1907, his condition had worsened to a great degree. In January, the *San Juan Prospector* in Del Norte stated that Bourquin and two other boys were burning a bonfire near the hospital when Roy "threw a [dynamite] cap into the fire which nearly destroyed the sight of an eye of another youngster. Bourquin has a mania for explosives and is constantly playing with them."[124] Just a few days later, Bourquin very nearly blew up the county hospital itself.

The former Teller County Hospital has functioned as a lovely hotel outside of Cripple Creek for many years. *Courtesy Cripple Creek District Museum.*

As it happened, residents at the Teller County Hospital and Poor House were sometimes called on to do odd jobs. One of them had gone down to the basement to light a fire in the boiler that heated the large, two-story structure and "happened to see the sticks [of dynamite] lying on top of the furnace," wrote the *San Juan Prospector*.[125] Had they been overlooked, the heat would have likely blown up the hospital and could have killed several people. County physician W.E. Driscoll, whose wife, Maggie, was the matron of the hospital, immediately questioned Bourquin. It took some time for him to admit that he had placed the dynamite on the furnace to dry it out. Dr. Driscoll pressed charges. Bourquin was arrested and taken to the Teller County Jail in Cripple Creek.

The *Rocky Mountain News* elaborated on Bourquin's condition. Dr. Driscoll verified that "the boy takes a delight in witnessing explosions and setting fire to property," also that he had been expelled from the State Industrial School some years before because "he was utterly helpless and was too much trouble." Although he could not wash or dress himself, Driscoll said, Bourquin was "not helpless when it comes to lighting a match. He has steel hooks for hands and with the sharp point of either of these he picks up a match, places it between his teeth and lights it against the wall. He has been known to carry dynamite in his pocket and it is said in handling the powder he forces one of the hooks into the stick, and how explosions were averted is beyond understanding. It is claimed that Bourquin has started several fires under buildings and the only reason he gives is that he likes to see the blaze."[126]

At the time, there was no help for Bourquin's condition. Although authorities concluded he had no relatives, apparently nobody knew about Bourquin's half sisters or Charles Bourquin, who had relocated to Yuma, Arizona. Having nowhere else to go, Bourquin was eventually allowed to return to the Teller County Hospital. In 1910, hospital staff assisted Bourquin in successfully applying for a portion of his father's Civil War pension. Although he was now in his twenties, the records documented him as a "helpless child."[127] But that description did not even begin to explain the complexities of Bourquin's pyromania disorder.

Bourquin remained at the Teller County Hospital for several more years, where the all-woman staff tried to look after him as best as they could. In 1913, the *Independence Daily Reporter* in Kansas published a "pitiful letter" to the editor on the front page. Bourquin had dictated the note to one

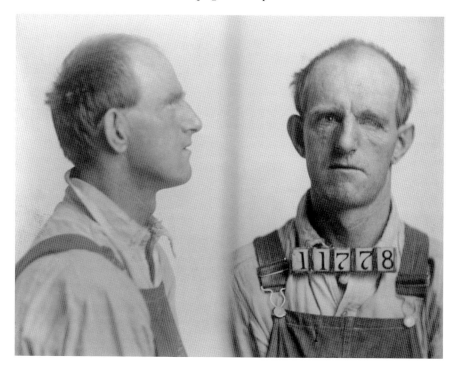

The long-ago injury to his eye is apparent in Bourquin's 1922 mug shot. *Courtesy Colorado State Archives.*

of the nurses. The letter inquired about Bourquin's half sister, Molly Bourquin, who had since married. "I don't know her name now," the letter explained, "but I was told she was in Independence, Kansas. I am her brother and have not seen her since I was a small child. I can't remember how she looks but I sure need her. I am at the County Hospital and I have my arms both off and am hurt in other ways, so if you will be kind enough to try and locate her I will be so thankful to you." The newspaper concluded the article by asking that "if anyone knows Miss Bourquin, please advise The

Reporter."[128] Unfortunately, Molly had not only changed her last name to Berkman (which her father also had done on occasion), but she had also married and now lived in Oklahoma. Bourquin's letter was never answered.

By 1917, Roy Bourquin was somewhat of an institution at the county hospital when he duly registered for the draft, even though he would obviously never serve in the military. Someone had filled out the draft card for him, but he signed it himself. "Wrote name with pencil between teeth," said a note attached to the card.[129] Five years would go by before Bourquin made the newspapers once again. This time, the charge was much more serious: statutory rape of a thirteen-year-old girl. Judge Arthur Cornforth showed no leniency and sentenced him to twenty years to life at the Colorado State Penitentiary in Cañon City, where he was enrolled as inmate no. 11778.

By the time of the 1940 census, Bourquin was back in Cripple Creek. Because the county hospital now functioned as a nursing home, the St. Nicholas Hospital, under matron Mabel Rutherford, had taken him in. The census indicates how little Mabel and her staff may have known about him: the census documents Bourquin as being born in Colorado, and nobody knew where his parents were born. The census also stated Bourquin was employed as a janitor. When he was required to register for the draft once again in 1942, Mabel Rutherford was named as his point of contact. She also likely assisted him when he applied for social security benefits.

Above: Among the newspapers to run the Ripley cartoon was the Durham, North Carolina *Herald Sun. Public domain.*

Opposite: Someone purchased a brand-new suit for Bourquin, which he wears while standing in front of the St. Nicholas Hospital. *Courtesy Cripple Creek District Museum.*

If Charles Bourquin ever contacted his brother, there is no record of it. It is interesting that when Charles died in California in 1946, he left behind his only child, Lindsay Boleyn Bourquin, who enjoyed a brief career as an actress in the years before her father died. Miss Bourquin had not only performed as an acrobat and dancer for the United Service Organization during World War II, but she also appeared in five films between 1930 and 1946—most notably a Three Stooges movie, *Gents Without Cents*. Did the actress even know about her notorious uncle Roy? Perhaps not, but at the very least, Bourquin was finally able to leave St. Nicholas Hospital. The 1950 census shows that for the first time, he was living unassisted in his own private home on the east side of Cripple Creek.

Yet another interesting fact about Bourquin was revealed in 1952, when the *Evening Vanguard* in California published a most intriguing tidbit: "Imagine the surprise of S. Brun Campbell, noted early day jazz piano player and known as 'The Ragtime Kid' in seeing a Ripley cartoon recently which told the story of his cousin, 'Hook' Roy Bourquin of Cripple Creek, Colo., who as a boy lost both his hands in a mine explosion and who has used hooks for hands ever since. The cartoon showed Bourquin shaving himself with his elbows. Campbell said he has not heard from his cousin in over a quarter century and he presumed he was dead."[130] The cartoon referenced in the story was from Ripley's Believe it or Not, a syndicated piece that ran regularly in newspapers across the country. The cartoon featuring Bourquin had appeared in January.

S. Brun Campbell (Sanford Brunson Campbell), it turned out, was the son of Bourquin's half sister Lulu, who had her own interesting story: In 1883, she was working as a maid for Luther "Lute" Campbell in Kansas. When Campbell's wife suddenly eloped that year, he married Lulu. Brun, as he was popularly known, was born the following year. The Campbells had left Kansas before Roy was even born, but Brun appears to have seen his younger uncle (not his cousin, as the *Evening Vanguard* claimed) on occasion and remembered him later. But Campbell had apparently not contacted Bourquin by the time he died in November 1952. His wife preceded him in death, and there were no children from the marriage. Any other surviving family had forgotten all about Roy Bourquin when he himself died in 1958. Rather than being deposited in the Potter's Field at Mt. Pisgah Cemetery, Roy was the beneficiary of some kind soul who purchased a plot for him in another area of the cemetery. Today, he has a simple wooden grave marker that is maintained by the City of Cripple Creek and is visible when driving into the cemetery. Few people passing by, however, know of Roy Bourquin as the onetime pyromaniac of Cripple Creek.

REDEMPTION FOR THE CRUMLEYS

*H*istory buffs of Cripple Creek are well versed on the death of mining millionaire Sam Strong, who was shot at the Newport Saloon in 1902 by Grant Crumley. The scandalous story has grown in proportion since it was first reported in newspapers, along with equally sordid tales about Crumley's brothers, Sherman and Newt. But were the Crumley brothers simply in the wrong place at the wrong time? Perhaps, and it may be refreshing to discover that the boys—well, Grant and Newt, anyway—managed to redeem themselves quite nicely after leaving Colorado. But they certainly did leave their mark in the annals of the Cripple Creek District.

The story of the Crumleys begins in Union County, Georgia, where their parents, Benjamin Jasper Crumley and Sarah Addington, had a total of ten children between 1855 and 1876. The three offspring that figure most prominently in this story are William A. "Sherman" Crumley, James Ulysses S. "Grant" Crumley and Newton "Newt" Crumley. Between 1880 and 1893, various family members moved to Kansas, then Oklahoma and finally, Colorado. In 1893, Grant and Sherman established the Crumley Brothers Carriage and Baggage Transfer Company in Colorado Springs. But the boys' efforts at running a legitimate business were seriously marred when Sherman became involved in the labor strikes at Cripple Creek during 1894.

At issue was the number of hours mine owners were forcing their employees to work for just three dollars per day. The miners asked for more pay and were turned down. That hardly seemed fair, since the district was booming, and the mine owners were growing increasingly rich. The biggest blow came in January 1894, when most of the mines announced that they were increasing the workday for their miners to nine, and even ten, hours without an increase in pay. Those miners who did not want to work for more than eight hours were told their pay would be docked fifty cents each day.

Enter Free Coinage Union No. 19 of the Western Federation of Miners (WFM), which a Scottish miner named John Calderwood organized in January 1893. Calderwood soon succeeded in forming unions at Victor, Anaconda, Altman and Cripple Creek. Before long, eight hundred miners had joined the WFM, which maintained that the workday should consist of no more than eight hours. The mine owners refused to listen, and in February around five hundred miners walked off the job. Things escalated quickly from there.

Within a few months, things were so heated that El Paso County sheriff Frank Bowers demanded that Colorado governor Davis H. Waite send in the Colorado State Militia. Bowers made things sound so bad that Waite allowed fifty special sheriffs to be deputized at Colorado Springs. When the WFM complained, Governor Waite claimed Bowers had told him a deputy had been killed, which was untrue. Violence seemed imminent. The state militia, headed by Adjutant General T.J. Tarsney, was eventually called to break up the strikers.

When Tarsney arrived in the district, he found only a bunch of disheartened but dedicated miners at the scene of the strike. Although he successfully talked the mine owners into standing down, his support of the miners' union remained in certain people's minds. On June 24, Tarsney was staying at the Alamo Hotel in Colorado Springs when he was summoned downstairs for a telephone call. It was a ruse. Instead, a group of men kidnapped the general and drove him to a remote spot north of the city, where he was stripped, tarred and feathered and left to walk to safety in the dead of night. Sherman Crumley was driving the hack that kidnapped the general.

Crumley later claimed he was merely asked to bring a hack to the Alamo and that once there, a man with a gun ordered him to wait as Tarsney was bodily carried out by some other men and loaded into the wagon. The armed man jumped in beside Crumley, stuck a revolver in his ribs and ordered him to drive to Austin's Bluff north of Colorado Springs. There, Crumley watched as Tarsney was assaulted. "Now you get," Crumley quoted one of the men as saying to Tarsney.[131] Crumley was released, but the Crumley Brothers Carriage and Baggage Transfer Company was pretty much done after that.

By March 1895, Sherman and Grant Crumley had moved to the Cripple Creek District. Grant, a respected member of Cripple Creek's BPOE Lodge No. 316, bartended at various saloons. Sherman, however, narrowly escaped being implicated in the robbery of the Florence and Cripple Creek train outside of Victor. In addition, they say, Grant would keep a lookout for wealthy men spending lots of money, especially those who were winning at the gambling tables. These would be reported to Sherman and his friends, who waited until the men were alone on the streets or perhaps cutting through an empty alley, before robbing them. The Crumley boys were soon rumored to be running around with all manners of outlaws.[132] But it was Sherman who was far more wicked than his brother.

In August 1897, stolen goods were recovered from Sherman's cabin at Spring Creek, located just on the outskirts of the district. The *Cripple Creek Morning Times* named Crumley and his pals, one known as Purdy and one Charles Ripley, as the three criminals "who have been responsible for many a depredation in this district for the past two years." The threesome had already been implicated in the theft of some saddles and harnesses. Cripple Creek sheriffs Frank Boynton and Tom McMahon found those and more stolen goods in another cabin near Crumley's home, known to be one of his "hiding places."[133] The following year, he was also arrested as part of a gang-related robbery.

Grant Crumley, meanwhile, appeared to be working toward a better life and reputation. He did, however, enjoy the company of Grace Carlyle, an Ohio native who first appeared in Cripple Creek around 1897. Grace worked in the red-light district on Myers Avenue. By the 1900 census, the lady, sometimes identified as Gladys, was employed at a brothel run by Eva Prince at 333 Myers Avenue. Prince had first partnered with Madam Pearl DeVere when the two first arrived at the district town of Gillett. By 1894, both had relocated to Cripple Creek, where they parted ways and were running separate houses of pleasure.

Grace was spunky, too. In November 1900, the *Victor Record* told of how the woman tried to end her life via a deadly dose of morphine. An unnamed doctor came to her aid and pumped her stomach. The issue for Grace seemed to be that the physician dared to save her life, and she refused to pay him. This may have been the incident during which author Marshall Sprague claims that Grace attempted to beat up the doctor. If that is so, the physician recovered and promptly sued Grace for his twenty-five-dollar service call. Whether he got it is unknown, but Grace made the papers again a few months later.

This time, George Kurt sued Grace for nonpayment of $2,500 in furnishings he sold her when she opened her own place on South Fourth Street. Kurt also requested damages in the amount of $500 after a failed attempt to reclaim the items himself. During that attempt, Kurt was ousted from the house by Grace and her male friends, sustaining damages to himself as well as his furniture. At the same time, another man, John Pennington, was suing Grace for $5,000. Pennington had accompanied Kurt to Grace's place that evening and threw a few punches himself. Although he was arrested in the fracas, he was later found not guilty. Now, he was claiming his reputation had been damaged, thus the lawsuit. Grace naturally countered Kurt and Pennington's suits with her own claim. The *Victor Record*'s headline for the article took a tongue-in-cheek slant in capital letters: "GRACE CARLYSLE SUES FOR $8,000. GRACE CARLYSLE SUED FOR $8,000."[134]

Was Grant Crumley at Grace's bordello when the fight broke out? Nobody knew, but the petite, pretty lady with the attitude problem did enjoy occasionally shedding her clothing atop Crumley's bar. At least she exhibited something close to social manners: one time, as a mine owner's wife was talking to Grant at work, Grace rushed to the bar and reprimanded her man for scratching his derriere in the presence of a lady. Grace is remembered too because on another occasion she was seen wearing an expensive evening gown by Ethel Carlton, the well-bred wife of millionaire Bert Carlton of the Colorado Trading and Transfer Company. Mrs. Carlton had given her cook several gowns to take to the Salvation Army as a donation. Instead, the cook sold the garments to the ladies along Myers Avenue. Grace was one of the lucky recipients, and it was Mrs. Carlton's dress she wore as the two passed each other on the street.

There may have been another reason Grant Crumley kept company with Grace Carlyle. His niece by his brother Charles, Lida, was taking an interest in the red-light districts of the Cripple Creek District. In 1899, Lida was living in Pueblo and renting furnished rooms at 1–2 South Union Avenue—very near the city's own red-light district. Although there is no solid evidence that Lida practiced prostitution at that early date, she did live in the district for a time, where it can be presumed that she learned the tricks of the trade from women like Grace Carlyle. Lida eventually moved to Prescott, Arizona, where she opened her own bordello. Daisy Ford, previously of Victor, followed Lida and worked for her. Between 1901 and 1907, Lida ran the largest brothel in town, and her love for diamonds earned her the nickname "Diamond Lida." Tragically, she suffered through a terrible divorce and lost everything before freezing to death in an abandoned car on a lonely road in 1939.[135]

By 1902, Grant Crumley had been running the roulette wheel at the prestigious National Hotel on Bennett Avenue for some time, with his own suite there to boot. When he was offered a job managing the Newport Saloon and Gambling Hall, Crumley jumped at the chance. The Newport was located just across Fourth Street from the National, in the bottom southwest corner of the Gold Mining Stock Exchange Building. Although the Newport's roulette table had been robbed at least twice in the recent past, Crumley's proprietorship kept the games honest to a great degree. Brothers Newt and Sherman were also gainfully employed: Newt worked as a clerk and lived at the Vassar Rooming House just a few doors from the National, while Sherman toiled as both a clerk and a miner.

When new laws outlawed nickel slot machines and required poker tables and roulette wheels to be kept away from the public eye, Grant Crumley acquiesced and did his best to run a clean, upscale house. After all, the Stock Exchange Building brought in loads of wealthy men with whom Crumley could make connections. One of them was Sam Strong, a former Colorado Springs lumberman who had struck it rich with his own mine just outside of Victor. One would think that with millions of dollars comes a sense of

The interior of the Newport Saloon as it looked during renovations in 1998. *Author's collection.*

decorum, but that was certainly not the case with Strong. He has been described as boisterous, rowdy, philandering and lots of other unkind words. Just after marrying his wife, Regina Neville, in 1900, Strong was sued by two other women who claimed he jilted them. And when he walked into the Newport late in the evening of August 21, 1901, Strong was very drunk.

Strong and Crumley already had an issue between them. Just a week before, Strong had run up a gambling debt of $2,500 and paid it by check. The next day, however, he claimed that Crumley's roulette wheel was crooked and stopped payment on his check. Crumley doggedly went after him, and the two settled on $200 to clear the debt. Now here Strong was in the Newport, in the company of his father-in-law, John Neville, a clerk named Clarence or John Fitch and attorney C.R. Prentice. Strong's companions were attempting to guide the drunken millionaire home, but the man insisted on gambling while throwing insults at Crumley.

Around midnight, word came that Sherman Crumley had just been shot in the leg by an employee of Strong's. Why Crumley was shot was unknown, but Strong began hooting, called him a "tinhorn" and made no secret that he thought the man got what he deserved. Grant kept his cool, and after a while, Sam Strong and his buddies wandered off. They came back around 6:00 a.m., and Strong played roulette. When Crumley poked his head into the gaming room to check on things, Strong, who was winning, bellowed, "Whatsa matter Grant? Running a straight wheel for a change?"[136]

Crumley calmly returned to the bar and was soon joined by Neville and Fitch. When Strong came in, Crumley was telling the men about the debacle over the $2,500 check. An infuriated Strong yelled, "Here, that's my daddy you're talking to!" Seconds later, the drunken millionaire pulled a revolver from his pocket. "Take your hands out of your pockets, Crumley," he shouted, "or I'll kill you!"[137] Neville and Fitch tried to keep Strong from firing his pistol while "Crumley, thinking his life was in danger, rushed behind the bar, picked up a sawed-off shotgun and discharged it at Strong, blowing off the top of his head," according to the *Victor Record*.[138] Then he carefully laid the shotgun on the bar.

Strong was still breathing. Neville ran to Shockey's Drugstore and phoned for an ambulance, and physicians J.F. Crane and John Hereford arrived at the scene. There being not much to do for Strong, he was taken to the Neville home, where he died a couple hours later. When the sheriff arrived, Crumley willingly went to the jail, where he requested a cigar and a shot of bourbon. "I shot Strong because if I hadn't, he would have shot me," he explained.[139] In the days that followed, investigators created a reenactment photo of Strong lying on the floor of the Newport as the coroner conducted an inquest. The story appeared in newspapers nationwide. Crumley bonded out for fifty dollars as the investigation continued. In November, he was acquitted of all wrongdoing. Not a soul blamed Crumley for killing Strong. "The community was shocked," acknowledged the *Victor Record*, "but, it must be admitted, the poignant grief and the surprised indignation which would have followed the violent death of many men so generally known, was largely lacking."[140]

Grant Crumley remained in Cripple Creek, working at the Newport and doing business with other prominent businessmen while living on East Masonic Avenue, just a block or two from his beloved Grace Carlyle. By early 1904, however, he and his brothers were ready to leave Cripple Creek. Their destination was Nevada, where gambling and mining prospects both looked good. With his experience at the National Hotel and the Newport Saloon under his belt, Crumley had no problem getting a job running the Palace, "one of the largest resorts of the west," in Reno.[141] When the city began cracking down on gambling, Crumley moved on to Goldfield.

As it happened, the mining town of Goldfield had just been established in 1903, and the president of the town site was a former Cripple Creek resident named Alva D. Myers. Another interesting note in history is that quite by coincidence, Myers Avenue in Cripple Creek and Myers Avenue in Goldfield each became home to their respective city's red-light district—although in Cripple Creek, Myers Avenue was named after city founder Julius Myers, while Goldfield's Myers Avenue was named for Alva Myers. It is doubtful that Grace Carlyle accompanied Crumley, but there were plenty of other delightful ladies in Goldfield to keep him company. Grant Crumley became especially well known in Goldfield, as well as in Tonopah twenty-seven miles away. He first bore mention in Tonopah during October 1904 as a principal shareholder and director in the Princeton Goldfield Mining Company. The next month, he partnered with a fellow Coloradoan, Hank Knight, in a saloon and gambling house.

Crumley was right in his element; by January 1905, the *Tonopah Bonanza* was regularly writing of his opinions regarding the boxing arena, as well as his continued mining investments. He was elected treasurer of the Knights of the Royal Arch lodge. He weathered a debacle in 1906 wherein Sheriff Thomas McMahon wrongfully implied that Grant had brutally killed two men. Younger brother Newt filed suit against the sheriff for tarnishing Grant's reputation and won. When Grant purchased sixty lots at the new town of Blair west of Tonopah and announced his plans to build a fancy hotel complete with twenty-eight suites, a clubroom, restaurant and bar, everybody was all for it.

Crumley purchased other real estate too. In November, he bought the Monte Carlo saloon in Tonopah and helped start the Pavilion Theater during 1907. He also married Katherine "Kate" Brown, who hailed from Texas. The townspeople thought a lot of the couple. When Kate had an attack of appendicitis at Blair in October, the *Tonopah Daily Bonanza* reported that a car was sent at breakneck speed to retrieve her personal physician. Efforts to save her were for naught, and she died at the couple's Tonopah home on October 16. She is buried in Reno.

Grant Crumley had no sooner buried his wife when Sherman got arrested for buying a bucket of beer in Tonopah and enticing two underage children to drink it until they were quite drunk—while their mother was attending the theater. The incident happened just days after Kate Crumley's funeral. Sherman was fined twenty dollars in the incident. Would he ever straighten up? Not hardly. Rather than join his brothers in their lucrative business deals, Sherman worked around Goldfield and Tonopah as a common laborer. When he wasn't causing trouble, he was laid up in bed with various illnesses, perhaps due to his drinking habits. When he died from a combination of alcoholism and exposure in 1921, his brothers sent his body back to Kansas for burial.

In the months after Kate Crumley's death, Grant began selling off his extensive properties. Also on the market was Crumley's Grand Hotel, a grocery store, the Cobweb Saloon and sixty thousand shares in the Tonopah Sewer and Drainage Company. The Blair Hotel and Crumley's beautiful home were among those that didn't sell, but it was soon obvious that the widower Crumley was not cashing out so he could leave; just after the Cobweb sold in December, Crumley's newest saloon, the Nevada Club, premiered in Tonopah's State Bank and Trust Building.

The *Daily Bonanza* described the place during a sneak peek on December 28, 1907: "Marble, mahogany, tiling, colored and clear art glass, mirrors and myriads of incandescent electric lamps, solid silver utensils, beautiful cut glass, an elaborate cosy [*sic*] corner, heavy bronze cuspidors, a handsome lunch counter and a massive safe with safe deposit vaults, are some of the effects which in combination disclose a work of art." Notable too is that over the diamond-dust mirror above the lunch counter was "a fine painting of Cheyenne Canyon, showing the road in the mountains leading from Colorado Springs to Cripple Creek."[142] Other amenities included a wine room, poker tables and a roulette wheel. The Nevada Club would swing its doors wide open on New Years Eve. In a review of the party, the *Daily*

Bonanza commented, "It were good for Tonopah if there were more Grant Crumleys [*sic*]."[143]

The Nevada Club was so successful on its first night that the very next day, Crumley was able to repurchase the Cobweb Saloon. Throughout 1908, the *Daily Bonanza* was rife with the rich stories that floated from the Nevada Club, like the time Julius Smith made a whopping seventy-seven bets that his wife would give birth to a boy, and she did. Smith collected $365 in bets and spent it all at the club, plus an additional $3. The Nevada Club's boxing matches were well attended. And when a big fire burned many businesses on May 12, including the Cobweb Saloon, Crumley was publicly thanked for helping direct people, wagons and horses out of harm's way. The day after the fire, everyone met at the Nevada Club to donate money and make plans for cleaning up the mess.

Where was Newt Crumley all this time? While Grant enjoyed being in the spotlight around Tonopah, Newt was spending much of his time on his own business interests in Reno. The only time he appeared in print was when he left Tonopah or returned, entertained a visiting family member or was involved in something alongside Grant. During 1908, for instance, it was reported that the Crumley brothers owned a mine at the budding camp of Silver Bow. At Christmas, they purchased numerous items at a church charity bazaar. In January 1909, Newt, normally a conservative bettor, put down $200 on his favorite at a boxing match in Goldfield. Anytime the Crumley brothers made a move, the *Daily Bonanza* reported on it.

The *Tonopah Daily Bonanza* featured several pictures of the Nevada Club in its January 3 issue. *Public domain.*

Portly Grant Crumley was often the subject of good-natured ribbing in the *Tonopah Daily Bonanza*. *Public domain.*

Grant Crumley continued blossoming into a real man of the town. Everybody liked him, and everybody supported him. The *Daily Bonanza* ribbed him by accusing him of trying to dig a tunnel to the beer keg at the ballpark so he wouldn't have to pay for a glass. Folks laughed heartily when he played the female lead in a performance of *Romeo and Juliet* at the Tonopah Elks in January. They teased him about how many valentines he received in February. They giggled when he placed an ad in the paper in May: "Wanted—100,000 men who understand repairing electric pianos…A steam beer to the winning contestant."[144] A few weeks later, Grant sold a half interest in the Nevada Club to Newt and continued investing in the local mines and even a railroad to Bodie, California. At Grant's house, which the brothers shared in the California Heights neighborhood of Tonopah, parties were frequent. The boys also attended various soirees downtown, and in December, Grant gladly concocted a wicked punch for the boys at the Elks Lodge. The *Daily Bonanza* duly noted that he was still a member of the Cripple Creek Elks Lodge in good standing.

News of the Crumleys during 1910 included Newt marrying Rosalia "Lee" Hunt of Belmont in March. In April, the Blair Hotel caught fire and burned to the ground. Grant was spending time in Reno when the *Reno Nevada Weekly* revealed the truth about his trip there: he was dating a mysterious femme, whom the newspapers dubbed the "Lavender Lady."[145] Who she was remains a mystery, but when two Oklahoma girls sent a letter to Reno looking for men to marry, the *Daily Bonanza* claimed Grant wrote back to them both and even requested photographs of them. The paper also teased, in October, that Grant had married. But he hadn't—yet.

For a while, nothing else was mentioned about Crumley's search for another wife. He did sell his interest in the Nevada Club in early 1911—right around the time he became an uncle to Newton Hunt Crumley Jr. Then in May, Newt Sr. received a telegraph from his brother in Reno reading, "Meet me at the train with a cab, as I have excess baggage." The *Daily Bonanza* heard about it, "smelled a rat" and contacted the *Reno Journal*. Sure enough, Grant had married again, to Lucy Lucretia Clow of New York. The couple returned to Tonopah as the newspaper wished them well.[146] After that, reporters appear to have let the Crumleys be. Although they were still wealthy, with a lot of business endeavors under their belt, they were now officially respectable, married men.

The Crumley boys remained highly successful. From 1923 to 1925, Newt owned and operated the elegant Goldfield Hotel in Goldfield with its 150 rooms, a lobby furnished with solid mahogany and an in-house orchestra. He also purchased the Commercial Hotel at Elko and expanded the facility to include gambling and the first high-end entertainment Nevada casinos would see. By 1930, Grant and Lucy Crumley had relocated permanently to Reno, where Grant was the president of the National Realty & Investment Company. He remained close to Newt, whose investments enabled him

The opulent Goldfield Hotel, once owned by Newt Crumley, is currently under restoration. *Author's collection.*

to send Newt Jr. to the University of Nevada and watch as the young man was commissioned as a second lieutenant in the Army Air Corps and completed a tour of duty before returning to Elko and the family business.

Grant and Lucy eventually moved to California, where Grant died in 1940 at the age of seventy-two. Newt Sr. followed in 1946 and was fondly remembered by many. Biographer and family friend Brian Tim Wellesley depicted Newt Sr. as a friendly man with a zest for life: "He grubstaked many a prospector; gave many a hungry man a handout, and his donations to charitable organizations and to the churches were always among the most generous."[147] It was left to Newt Jr. to carry on his father's work by completing a second hotel, the Ranch Inn, in Elko. He also was appointed as commander of Minto Air Force Base and became a state senator of Nevada.

Newt Crumley Sr. is still fondly remembered by his descendants and friends to this day. *Courtesy of Tim Wellesley.*

Wellesley and a friend of the family who attended school with one of Newt Jr.'s daughters recalled a family man with very high standards. The friend also remembered that the nightclub acts at both of Crumley's hotels included a Saturday matinee for the schoolchildren of Elko. "I suppose some of the comics had trouble cleaning up their act for a bunch of kids," she commented.[148] After many years of offering fine hotel and casino entertainment, Newt Crumley Jr. and his wife, Frances, moved to Reno. In 1957, they purchased the Holiday Hotel and added a casino floor. Tragically, Crumley died in a plane accident in 1962, just thirty miles from his birthplace. His death marked the end of the official reign of the Crumley boys in Colorado and Nevada. Today, Newt Sr.'s descendants continue to reside in Nevada on property their ancestors purchased back when they were the popular, well-loved kings of the gaming world.

THE MOST HATED MAN IN THE CRIPPLE CREEK DISTRICT

*O*f all the wicked men who passed through the Cripple Creek District in its day, James A. Warford rates among those who were disliked the most. He was born in Iowa before the family moved to Missouri in 1868. In his early twenties, Warford married his second cousin, Sarah Adaline "Addie" Rhoades, and in about 1894 the couple set out for Colorado. Two daughters came from the union: Mable, born in 1895 soon after the Warfords reached the Centennial State, and Theodosia, born in 1896. The couple was in Montrose in 1897 when Warford was convicted of "malicious mischief."[149] Details of his crime are unknown, but it was serious enough to merit sentencing Warford to eighteen months in the penitentiary. It was also rumored that in his youth, Warford had gone by an alias, "Jim Lambert."[150] What he did under that name is unknown, but he was out of jail by 1900 when the family was living in Telluride. On the same day the census was taken, June 26, Addie gave birth to a third daughter, Freda.

By 1902, there were troubles in the Warford family. After seven-year-old Mable died, the grieving family relocated again, this time to Colorado City—the rowdy little town west of Colorado Springs. There, a disconsolate Addie once attempted to end her life in nearby Garden of the Gods. A short time later, the Warfords moved to the district, where the second labor war in a decade was warming up. At issue was the eight-hour workday, which the Colorado Supreme Court approved in 1902 following pressure from the Western Federation of Miners union. The trouble was that by

1903–4, many mine owners in the district were refusing to abide by the law and requiring their employees to work longer hours for the same pay. In response, roughly 1,750 union miners walked off the job. Skirmishes and violence quickly followed.

In the coming months, striking miners were pitted against strikebreakers in several violent engagements that included arrests, threats, beatings and shootouts. At one point, Governor James H. Peabody, who sided with the mine owners, declared martial law and approved of deporting striking miners from the district. As an employee of the Golden Cycle Mine, as well as the Mine Owners Protective Association (MOA), Warford sided with the mine owners. Professional assassin Harry Orchard, however, did not. When Orchard managed to blow up the train depot at the town of Independence and kill the men hired to replace the strikers, it made Warford madder than he already was. To make things worse, a heated election was on the horizon. Peabody's reelection was on the ballot.

To ensure the voting went smoothly, Teller County officials hired several temporary deputies to oversee the polling stations. Warford and a co-worker, Thomas Brown, were accordingly deputized to oversee the voting booths at Goldfield. Three local constables were posted there as well. But the officials apparently did not know, or perhaps did not care, that two of them, Isaac Leabo and Chris Miller, were vehemently opposed to the MOA, nor that

Harry Orchard's blowing up the Independence Depot made James Warford so mad he could shoot somebody. *Courtesy Cripple Creek District Museum.*

Warford had only recently responded to his disagreement with a news article that sided with the miners by wrecking the newspaper office and shooting a clock on the wall.

Come voting day, Leabo and Miller arrived at Goldfield and positioned themselves on a nearby fence. Believing they were there to make trouble, Warford immediately walked over and told the men, "We want you to get away from here."[151] Things quickly escalated from there, and Miller pulled his gun. Warford was faster, however, and shot Miller in the neck. Leabo tried to pull out his revolver too, and Warford shot him. The bullet entered his shoulder and penetrated his neck as well. Ike Spencer, who knew the men, heard the commotion and ran out of his house carrying a Winchester rifle but was quickly subdued. Miller died within twenty minutes. Leabo also died following an operation trying to save him.

Warford, Brown and Spencer were all arrested and taken to jail in Victor. Sentiments ran high, especially since Leabo and Miller were both married with children. Before long, rumors began that the killing of the two men was premeditated, that both had been shot in the back and that Warford and Brown had been hired by the MOA. Although the coroner's jury determined that Warford had shot his victims in self-defense, Judge Cunningham denied the killer's bond. Only Brown was allowed to bond out. Warford languished in jail until his trial in March 1905. The trouble was nobody appeared to have witnessed him shooting Leabo and Miller. And although the labor strikes had been somewhat settled, there was still a lot of dissension in the district. It really should have been no surprise that the jury took an excruciating sixty-seven hours in deliberation, ending with a hung jury. Warford was a free man, but he continued to make trouble.

On May 16, Warford was back to work at the Golden Cycle when he, Walter Kenley and John Chapman accosted Sheriff Sherman Bell and his deputy, Thomas Underwood, right in the middle of downtown Cripple Creek. Kenley and Chapman had only recently been released from jail. They, along with Warford, began demanding their guns, which were still locked up at the county jail. The men started marching Bell and Underwood to the jail at gunpoint, until they realized they were standing out in public. The men quickly changed course and began marching the officers toward Anaconda instead. A posse soon located the party near the Gold Bond Mine. Officers fired warning shots in the air. Kenley returned fire but got whacked over the head by Underwood. Warford was so surprised that he tripped and went tumbling down the hill, hitting his head.

Goldfield, the way it looked around the time of the murders of Chris Leabo and Chris Miller. *Courtesy Cripple Creek District Museum, CCDM #169.*

The ex-convicts were taken back to the county jail. An angry mob formed a lynch party but was prevented from doing anything by Bell. At their trial in October, only Warford and Kenley were found guilty of assault with intent to kill Bell and sentenced to prison. And in December, a second trial against Warford in the killing of Issac Leabo resulted in the verdict of murder. This time, Warford was sentenced to life in prison at the state penitentiary. Addie Warford eventually filed for divorce and remarried.

That might have been the end of Warford's murderous career but for Governor Henry Buchtel, who issued pardons for Warford and Kenley in 1908. Naturally that did not sit well with Warford's adversaries. Within a year, he was on trial for the third time over killing Leabo and Miller. This time, due to the amount of media exposure and hard feelings in the district, Warford's attorneys successfully submitted a request for a change of venue to Cañon City. When no bondsman came forward to spring Warford, Judge Cavendar released him on his own recognizance. Perhaps the judge was exhibiting sympathy, seeing as Warford's daughter Freda had just died.

Nothing ever came of Warford's trials for murder. But plenty of men around the district remembered the man's dastardly deeds and were determined to reckon with him. In February 1912, two bombs were found in the basement of Warford's home, which had been set on fire. The explosives were large enough that had they exploded, the firemen at the scene would have likely been killed. Two men, William Edwards and Frank Russ, were jailed in connection with the deed, their motives left unexplained by newspapers.

Efforts to blow up James Warford's house may have failed, but someone obviously wanted the man dead and did not stop until the deed was done. On April 17, a prospector named Gus Franks found Warford's body on Battle Mountain near the Portland Mine. The gruesome details were published in newspapers: Warford had been shot in the side of the face and twice in the stomach. After the man fell face down on the ground, another bullet was delivered to the back of his head. Yet another shot severed part of his left ear, and a final shot hit him in the back and pierced his heart. The bullets from Warford's body showed that three different guns were used. Near the body were two sacks containing three bombs made with dynamite that were big enough to kill anyone within a radius of two hundred feet had they gone off.

Who murdered James Warford? Edwards and Russ were immediately suspected, but there wasn't enough evidence to convict them. Also, someone had pawned Warford's Colt .45 revolvers—under the dead man's name—in Colorado Springs on April 11. A Victor undertaker took charge of the body as rumors circulated that Warford's buddies in life included the notorious assassin Tom Horn. And even Warford's family declined to claim his corpse or send money for his burial.

On April 20, James Warford was interred at Victor. "The body was taken to Sunnyside cemetery in the common dead wagon," explained the *Rocky Mountain News*, "fear being expressed that in case a hearse was used, sentiment would be expressed in a public demonstration by the miners." One of the only two people in attendance, Reverend Gatewood Milligan, spoke a few words over the grave for "less than five minutes."[152] The only other person present was the undertaker. A kindly banker from Missouri,

126—PORTLAND MINE —CRIPPLE CREEK DISTRICT.

The locale where James Warford's bullet-riddled body was found. *Author's collection.*

identified as R.E. Maupin, paid the burial expenses. Even today, Warford's grave is unmarked.

During the investigation into Warford's mysterious death, District Attorney Joseph Furgerson questioned six possible witnesses. Nobody knew anything. More questions popped up when Warford's personal belongings were discovered to include a belt buckle engraved "Deputy Sheriff of the Black Hills," as well as a law officer's badge from Elkhorn, Nevada. Verification of his employment in South Dakota came from the *Lead Daily Call*, which confirmed that Warford lived there for a time and lived as "a quiet and peaceful man."[153] The newspaper's opinion differed from that of the *Deadwood Pioneer Times*, which commented, "He was a deputy sheriff in the Black Hills and bore a bad reputation and seemed to enjoy it."[154] Whether Warford was employed in Nevada remains unverified.

The burial of James Warford did not end his story. In July, the *Cañon City Record* published a most curious article. Although James Warford was identified by those who knew him and some receipts in his pockets bearing his name, there was now a question as to whether the man found on Bull Hill really was him. Apparently, there was a story floating around that Warford's youngest brother, Columbia Warford, had just recently heard from fourteen-year-old Theodosia Warford. The last surviving child of James Warford told her uncle that she knew her father was alive and well in Alaska. Was Theodosia told a fib to save her from grief? Or did James Warford fake his own death and live happily ever after under an assumed name in Alaska? Nobody knows, and they likely never will.

THE STORY OF A MURDERED MISTRESS

An old proverb goes, "Hell hath no fury like a woman scorned." That was certainly true of Martha "Mattie" Vidler, who caught her husband, Sam, red-handed—along with his paramour of the moment—at Cripple Creek's opulent National Hotel. Sam was a British-born army veteran who first came to America in 1888. The following year, he married Mattie, the daughter of a shoemaker from St. Louis, Missouri. Their first child, Walter, was born in 1891. A second son, Sam Jr., was born a few years later in Colorado.

Vidler was first mentioned by newspapers during the early 1890s, when he was managing the Cheyenne Mountain Country Club in Colorado Springs and rubbing elbows with the city's wealthy men. The job was perfect for him since he loved sports and frequently participated in athletic events. By 1895, the Vidlers had moved to the district town of Gillett, where Sam worked as an advisor for promoter Joe Wolfe in preparation for the ill-fated bullfight that occurred on the edge of town that August. A year later, Vidler was employed as Gillett's city clerk while editing the town's newspaper, the *Gillett Gazette*. The trouble was, Sam Vidler could sometimes be on the shady side of shady. In April 1897, for instance, James Parfet ran for mayor of Gillette. O.W. Keith won instead. The loser Parfet filed suit, claiming that Sam had bullied the election officials into counting five illegal votes against him.

The Vidlers soon moved to Cripple Creek, where, by the fall of 1897, Sam was an editor for the *Cripple Creek Citizen*. He and Mattie were mentioned regularly in society pages, and he was elected vice president of the Cripple

The Gillett bullfight, seen here on the second day, when few were in attendance. *Courtesy Cripple Creek District Museum.*

Creek Press Club. By 1899 he was working for the *Cripple Creek Morning Record*, and the family now lived in a nice home on West Golden Avenue. Vidler's name continued appearing in Colorado newspapers as he pursued his love of foot racing and other sports. When Mattie gave birth to her third child, Dorothy, in 1903, Vidler seemed to consider it a personal victory. Sam Vidler had become everybody's everyman. He was popular, and he was powerful. And he knew it.

Vidler continued dabbling in politics in his own menacing way. It was he who, during the 1904 labor strikes, once joined a committee to overthrow the government at the city of Victor, the hard way. Anti-strikers had just gotten the entire staff of the *Victor Record* newspaper arrested for sympathizing with striking miners. The committee, "composed of Sam Vidler, Frank Pinson, Dr. McCowan, J. Gaffney and an old soldier named Harcourt," visited Justice of the Peace C.M. Harrington. Vidler himself held a gun on the judge and politely asked for his resignation. The judge acquiesced without further violence.[155] The strike was eventually settled, and Vidler went back to his work as a news correspondent.

All seemed well until April 1905, when the *Boulder Daily Camera* revealed that "Mrs. Vidler and her husband, who is the local correspondent for various newspapers and one of the Republican leaders, have been estranged for the past two months."[156] The *Florence Daily Tribune* followed up by reporting that Mattie "is said to have been extremely jealous" of her husband.[157] The

Rocky Mountain News explained even further: "Vidler has been living at the National hotel for the past two months. A domestic difficulty occurred at his home on the return of his wife from St. Louis two months ago. Gossips told her that her husband was unfaithful while she was away and she mentioned the fact to him. He left the house, which is on East Eaton Avenue, and went to the hotel to live."[158]

At issue was Vidler's cavorting with Helen Coulter Douglas. Back in 1904, the lady had told others that she was in Cripple Creek "on newspaper business in regard to the depot explosion at Independence June 6." A man named E.W. Sullivan later verified that "after the deportation train of June 20 had been sent out he was introduced to the woman by General Bell and asked to take her to the scene of the explosion so she could gather data. Although he never saw the woman afterwards, he is positive of the identification."[159] What Helen Douglas did not reveal was that the real reason she was in Cripple Creek in 1905 was to testify regarding the kidnapping of little Cecil Moats by his mother, Birdie Moats, on March 31.

What did Helen Coulter Douglas have to do with a mother kidnapping her own son? It just happened that Birdie Moats's sister was the famed madam Laura Bell McDaniel. Since the early 1890s, Laura Bell had run two different elegant brothels in the bawdy district of Colorado City, west of Colorado Springs. Unlike many women in her profession, Laura Bell was fortunate that her sister and mother supported her efforts, and the money she made enabled them to enjoy the finer things in life. In 1898, Birdie had married Edward Moats, whose sister was the wife of noted saloon owner Byron Hames. Cecil, their only child, was born in 1900. But by 1905, the Moatses' marriage was falling apart.

In the divorce decree against his wife, Moats was given custody of Cecil when he pointed out that Birdie Moats was "not a fit person to have the custody of the little son on account of alleged immoral associates."[160] The immoral associates included Laura Bell, who happened to be in Cripple Creek hoping to open a new brothel. A frantic Birdie Moats had taken her son and fled to Cripple Creek to see her sister before going to the West Coast for a time. She had returned to Colorado City in March, at which time her mother had taken Cecil to the police station to be returned to his father. Birdie was arrested. Helen Douglas knew about all of this because at the time, she was employed by Laura Bell at her Colorado City parlor house.

The *Rocky Mountain News* learned that it was while Helen was in Cripple Creek that she met Sam Vidler. Soon after he moved to the National Hotel,

Part of Laura Bell McDaniel's fancy parlor house in Old Colorado City is now a rest home. *Author's collection.*

Mattie Vidler met the woman as well: she happened to see Sam and Helen walking down the street together. Later, when Mattie saw Sam alone, she asked him to go to the house and talk to young Walter, who had misbehaved in school and was consequently severely beaten by his teacher. Sam went, but Mattie began looking for Helen Douglas and soon found her. Mattie walked right up to Helen. "Are you the woman who has come between me and my husband?" she asked. Helen replied, "You must be mistaken. I don't know your husband."[161]

Nothing else was said between the women, but Mattie knew that Helen Douglas was at the root of her marital troubles. The next morning, Mattie, "laboring under an awful mental strain and no doubt…temporarily deranged at the time from the grief she suffered because of the alleged unfaithfulness of her husband," visited the newspaper office to draw Sam's pay.[162] Then she proceeded along Bennett Avenue, where she purchased a revolver on her way to the National Hotel. Later, Mattie would say that she only meant to talk to her husband about Walter. She knew which room her husband occupied, but when she knocked, there was no answer. Returning to the lobby, Mattie peeked at the hotel register. Helen Douglas was staying in room 336.

Mattie went to Helen's door and knocked. Sam Vidler later explained what happened next:

> *Mrs. Douglas went to the door and inquired "Who's there?" No answer came, but at the same moment the door began to open slowly. Mrs. Douglas turning to me said I had better get into a closet.* [This I did,] *leaving the door open a little. A second later, hearing a shot fired, I pushed the door open and saw Mrs. Douglas stagger to the bed and fall backwards and my wife standing a few feet away with the smoking revolver in her hand. I said to her, "You see what you have done." She answered that she had not intended to kill the woman, but only to frighten her; but I told her it would have been far better if she had shot me. I then walked over to the bed and saw at a glance that Mrs. Douglas was dead, the bullet having entered the heart. I turned and wrested the revolver from my wife's hands and placed it in my hip pocket. A moment later Judge Brady walked into the room, and I handed him the gun.*[163]

The opulent National Hotel, where millionaire Winfield Scott Stratton had his own suite and Mattie Vidler shot the harlot Helen Douglas. *Courtesy Cripple Creek District Museum.*

Dr. A.C. Magruder was summoned from the Teller County Hospital, but there was nothing to be done for Helen Douglas. When Deputy Sheriff Thomas Underwood got to the hotel, he had no choice but to arrest Mattie Vidler as coroner George Hall took Helen's body to the morgue. Sam Vidler was taken alongside his wife to the county jail, where he admitted to the coroner's jury that he had gone to Helen Douglas's room the previous night. Mattie, meanwhile, "expressed the deepest regret, and when she referred to the probable consequences of her act, she gave way to tears. 'I don't so much care for myself, for I was miserable and unhappy since my husband left me; but I can't bear the thought of my three little children. The shame will [be] on them when they grow up and that is enough to break my heart. I love my children and my husband, but he made me unhappy by his attentions to other women.'"[164] The jury concluded that Mattie was temporarily insane when she shot Helen Douglas and allowed her to bond out of jail to the tune of $5,000. Local merchants gathered the money on her behalf.

Newspapers scrambled to find out more about Helen Douglas. The *Rocky Mountain News* described her as "the divorced wife of an English naval officer [who] had advantages and social position when a bride that were far removed from the life she has been leading in the West these ten years past."[165] Upon her arrival from New York around 1895, Helen spent some time in Denver's demimonde before making a circuit among various mining camps. Ironically, the *Florence Daily Tribune* claimed that in 1900 Helen "came into public notice in Denver in a downtown rooming house where she had followed her husband and another woman."[166] By 1902, Helen was working for Laura Bell McDaniel. The *Rocky Mountain News* could not resist adding that Helen "was a victim of the morphine habit and addicted to other drugs that helped her on her downward path."[167]

The papers also said that Laura Bell and Helen had often traveled to and from Cripple Creek together. During 1905, Laura Bell lived part time at the Waldorf House on Fourth Street. For about a year or two, she also ran her own brothel on Myers Avenue. She was also the only one who knew Helen Douglas well enough to speak about her to reporters. "I hardly know what to say about her," said the madam, "as she always impressed me as being a woman whose early life had been led in the midst of refinement. She was a great reader. She would say very little about her former life, but we were given to understand that she had traveled extensively and been all over the world."[168]

The kindhearted madam took charge of Helen's remains. Along with two of her employees, she "selected an expensive casket and arranged for the funeral" before purchasing a burial plot for Helen in Cripple Creek's Mt. Pisgah Cemetery. On a final note, reported the *Rocky Mountain News*, "Laura Belle [*sic*] said she would make no attempt to have Mrs. Vidler punished."[169] The madam also closed her business in Cripple Creek. Although Laura Bell never did business in Cripple Creek again, she did continue to visit her sister Birdie, who remarried to a respectable wallpaper dealer named Harry Hooyer in 1907. The Hooyers' son, Harry Jr., later graduated from Cripple Creek High School and attended prestigious Colorado College in Colorado Springs, on tuition money that was no doubt supplied by his infamous aunt's estate.

As for Sam and Mattie Vidler, they somehow managed to overcome the killing of Helen Douglas and were able to reconcile their marriage. The 1910 census finds them living together with their children, and Sam remained employed as a newspaper reporter. By 1920, they had moved to Denver, where Vidler was editor of the *Daily Mining and Financial Record*. After Mattie died in 1927, Vidler moved to Golden and dabbled in real estate. In 1934, he went to Gallup, New Mexico, to visit his daughter and perhaps never returned to Colorado. He died in 1942 in Arizona. Neither Mattie Vidler nor Helen Douglas have marked graves today.

"PRETTY JACK" McEACHERN, THE BODY SNATCHER

On January 24, 1906, the news broke that a former resident of Leadville, miner John Joseph McEachern, had died in a premature explosion of dynamite while working in the Three Jacks Tunnel on Straub Mountain in the Cripple Creek District. His death was not unusual, since it was widely known that the job of a miner could be mighty dangerous back then, compared to today's standards. Safety regulations were minimal and quite primitive. Falling rocks, falls, dangerous fumes or a miscalculated dynamite blast could have agonizingly fatal results. Sadly, such mishaps took place often, with deathly results.

A Nova Scotia native, McEachern had been in Colorado since the early 1880s. He was living in Leadville in 1889, and in 1898 he married his wife, Bessie Doig, in Colorado Springs. Three children came of the union. The two were back in Leadville when, for the second time, a fire burned their home. The house was insured for $1,000, and the family had only recently left Leadville with McEachern's partner, a sometime boxer, bartender and former policeman named John Crowley. The group soon arrived in Victor and found a suitable house on South Third Street. For reasons known only to themselves, McEachern and his wife repeated their marriage vows on July 22, 1905. And now McEachern was dead.

Victor undertaker George Hall was notified of McEachern's death. He duly went to the Three Jacks Tunnel with two employees and gathered what was left of the body, which was pretty much just a grisly pile of bones and flesh. Just a few days before McEachern died, another miner named

Leadville, Colorado, the way it looked when the McEacherns lived there. *Courtesy New York Public Library, G90F043-014ZF.*

Bob Speed had died after being crushed by a large rock in the Portland Mine. Some of the folks in attendance at McEachern's funeral in Sunnyside Cemetery passed by the grave of Speed. What a coincidence it was that that John McEachern had been one of the pallbearers at the dead man's funeral. Now, McEachern was dead and poor Bessie was a widow. When she moved to a new house on North Fifth Street shortly after burying her husband, folks just figured the move was an attempt to lower her rent.

Luckily, McEachern had thought to buy insurance before he died, and there would be money coming to support his family. On February 9, a postal worker appeared at Bessie's kitchen door with three life insurance checks for $1,000 each. As the postman knocked on the door, he peered through the window to see if the widow was there. Instead, the man nearly fainted when he saw John McEachern himself sitting at the table. The two locked eyes for a few seconds before the surprised postman dropped the checks, spun around and hightailed it to the sheriff's office to report what he saw. The postman was certainly not crazy, and the officers quickly grew suspicious. A group of them hastened to Bob Speed's grave at Sunnyside Cemetery, immediately noticed how the flowers on top of the burial were strewn about and dug up the grave. Speed wasn't in it.

The following day, officers visited the McEachern house but could not find the "dead" man. He was soon located, however, hiding out at the house of Bessie's neighbors Frank and Sarah Maudlin. Constable Harry Guyton knocked on the door and distinctly heard someone moving around inside. The officers broke down the door in time to see McEachern trying to make his escape. Guyton fired a warning shot, grazing McEachern ever so slightly across the chest. He, along with Frank Maudlin and Jack Crowley (who sometimes went by Jack Varley), were hauled to jail. It was Crowley who related how John McEachern had indeed faked his own death by digging up Bob Speed and blowing his body up in the Three Jacks Tunnel.

As the facts came forth, George Hall buried Bob Speed for a second time, in a much nicer spot in the Catholic section of Sunnyside Cemetery. Hall could not know that Speed's wife, who was not Catholic, would vehemently object to her husband being buried there. Poor Speed was dug up a second time and buried for the third time in the Protestant section. Meanwhile,

McEachern's crime was splashed all over the front page of the *Victor Daily Record. Public domain.*

stories about McEachern's dastardly deed began circulating through newspapers around the state. People now looked back on his house fires in Leadville and how there were whispers that the man had set them himself. The *Durango Democrat* even dug around and discovered that the insurance company refused to pay McEachern for the loss of the second house. The *Leadville Herald Democrat* also revealed that McEachern sported a nickname, "Pretty Jack."[170]

As McEachern's story gathered steam, groups of angry citizens started talking of lynching the man. The papers called him a "body snatcher," as well as several other names.[171] Officers removed the prisoner to safer quarters at the Teller County Jail in Cripple Creek as the story unfolded even more. Evidence gathered at the Three Jacks Tunnel revealed a shredded pair of miner's trousers and other items, but most telling was a piece of Speed's skull bearing black hair. There was red hair at the scene as well, and it belonged to McEachern. The wily man had been careful to nip off some of his own locks and stick them to the body before setting off the explosion. But he had not been careful enough.

Somewhere in Victor's Sunnyside Cemetery lies the thrice-buried body of Bob Speed. *Author's collection.*

Another piece of the puzzle was discovered too. It turned out that Sarah Maudlin was Bessie McEachern's sister. The ladies were immediately arrested, and it was discovered that they had $2,200 in cash. Some of it was sewn into Bessie's hat and a corset. More money was stashed in a baby carriage. A sobbing Bessie denied everything, claiming that she knew nothing of her husband's supposed fake death. But both women had recently been seen departing for Colorado Springs with their children, six in all, and several trunks in tow. Colorado Springs authorities soon discovered that the children had been left with an unnamed woman in a rented house at 531 East Bijou Street. That lady had lots of money on her as well. As the investigation continued, yet another person was arrested in connection with John McEachern's crime. His name was Lute Kellogg, and it was he who had assisted Bessie McEachern in filing the life insurance claim with Northwestern Mutual Insurance Company. A search of Kellogg's cabin revealed some forged notes, including one bearing the letterhead from the opulent National Hotel in Cripple Creek. Northwestern soon filed suit against the McEacherns for $3,918.79.

Bessie and Sarah were allowed to return to the McEachern house, where they remained under house arrest. Of the money Bessie received, there was $2,740 left. This was paid to Marshal H.A. Naylor, who in turn gave it to the local Northwestern agent. But Bessie still maintained that her husband was dead and that only by seeing him in the flesh could her mind be changed. Her demand was apparently denied. Frank Maudlin was released on bail as John McEachern was taken to Colorado Springs for trial, since everyone at the Teller County Courthouse agreed that public sentiment against the man might result in violence.

McEachern's trial began in March, where it was revealed that George Hall also had seen the man after he supposedly died. Hall testified that when he went to the Maudlin home to collect a bill for McEachern's "burial," he was shocked to see McEachern casually snoozing in bed. McEachern jumped up, Hall said, and stuffed a wad of money into his hand with instructions to "Take that and keep still."[172] The money amounted to $450, which Hall gave the authorities when he reported what happened the next day. Lute Kellogg also testified that he received a promissory note from McEachern and some money from Bessie McEachern for his part in the scheme.

On March 10, the jury rendered their decision in the case against McEachern, who sat in the courtroom with his young baby on his knee in hopes of gaining some sympathy. But guilty he was, and guilty he was found. Only then did McEachern confess to everything, but he also named

Kellogg, Crowley and Hall as his co-conspirators. It was Hall, McEachern said, who talked him into using a real body instead of a cow carcass, and that he had no idea whose body had been blown up. McEachern's statements were enough to reopen the investigation as an incensed Hall demanded to be arrested and asked that John and Bessie McEachern's statements be revisited. Officials agreed. Hall immediately bonded out as the *Rocky Mountain News* assured the public that "nearly everybody feels he has been made the victim of a foul slander."[173]

A week or so later Hall was naturally found not guilty. On March 23 the McEacherns, the Maudlins, Kellogg and Crowley were found guilty of "conspiracy to defraud and obtain money under false pretenses."[174] McEachern and Crowley were each sentenced to the Colorado State Penitentiary for nine and a half years. Nothing more was heard of them until August 1908, when McEachern's three-year-old son died unexpectedly. Deputy Warden Allan Jamieson was kind enough to bring him up to Victor for the funeral and allowed him to stay the night before taking him back to Cañon City the next day.

McEachern's brief taste of freedom slowly but surely gnawed at him. When Crowley applied for a pardon and was denied in January 1909, it squelched McEachern's idea of doing the same thing. Instead, he managed to escape while at a convict camp near Pueblo in June. He was on the lam for nearly five months before being apprehended in Bisbee, Arizona. Back in prison, McEachern boasted that he had traveled through Mexico and as far as Uruguay before taking a job at a mine in Bisbee.

There is no record of just when McEachern was finally released from prison, but records do show that Bessie divorced her husband in 1913. In 1914, McEachern was sentenced to Leavenworth Prison in Kansas, this time for counterfeiting. His plea for a pardon in 1916 apparently worked, for in 1917 he married Leona Wilson in Denver. Unfortunately, however, Leona died during the 1918 influenza epidemic in Leadville. A year later, McEachern was arrested again in 1919 at the town of Granite for bootlegging whiskey. McEachern was taking the hooch to Leadville.

When the *San Miguel Examiner* in Telluride heard about McEachern's arrest, the paper revealed that McEachern had recently been arrested there for bootlegging too. He had paid a fine and was told he could evade jail time if he promised to stay out of the county forever more. Instead of keeping his promise, however, McEachern "conceived the idea that the Telluride authorities were a set of boobs and that he could work them if he wanted to, so two weeks ago or such a matter he turned up here again like a bad penny." That time, said the paper, "he was taken to the courthouse and told that he [could] do one of the two things—beat it out of here or serve his jail sentence." McEachern wheedled that he was finishing up a big painting and wallpaper job for legitimate money. Officials were perhaps a bit too lenient when they told him he had a day to finish and leave town or go to jail. "He is the gink who served a penitentiary sentence some years ago," the paper concluded in disgust.[175]

For a few years, McEachern found legitimate work as a miner around Paradox in Montrose County, but in 1925 he was arrested yet again, for counterfeiting in White Pine County, Nevada. The *Rocky Mountain News*, which never seemed to tire of writing about him, rehashed the story of McEachern's fake death in the Cripple Creek District and mentioned that one time, while being brought from Utah to Leadville to face burglary charges, he escaped by jumping from the train while still wearing handcuffs.

When McEachern returned to Leadville for a final time, he was getting up in years. Whatever he did to make his way is unknown, although some would say it probably had to do with relieving someone else of their hard-earned cash. When he died in 1938, he was buried in Leadville's Evergreen Cemetery. Unlike others of his kind, McEachern's grave is marked today with a small metal tombstone. But there is nothing else to indicate that McEachern was once among the greatest swindlers that Colorado would ever see.

MEXICAN JENNIE

A Quilted Autobiography

He bought me a red velvet dress,
and I began working out of a crib on Meyers Street [sic],
with a narrow bed, a wooden crate
an oil lamp painted with hibiscus flowers.
The men called me
Mexican Jenny
because there were so many Jennys,
girls like me.[176]

Were she alive today, Jennie Wenner would likely be surprised to learn that people have been reading her story for years and years. Born to a German father and Mexican mother in Trinidad, near the New Mexico border between 1878 and 1880, Jennie first officially appeared on record in Colorado in 1901 when she married Edgar Keif. The marriage record gives her last name as Benton. Twenty-two-year-old Edgar Keif's name was recorded as Edward when he was found toiling as a miner at Swede Gulch on Gold Hill in the district in the 1900 census. How he met Jennie is unknown.

The Keif marriage did not last very long. In 1902, the couple relocated to Idaho Springs, where Edgar went to work in the Old Stag Tunnel. On September 9, he met his end when some dynamite exploded prematurely. Following his burial in Denver's Riverside Cemetery, the widow Jennie returned to Cripple Creek. In 1904, she met and married again to miner

Raymond E. Wenner, in Victor. Within a year, however, the Wenners had left Cripple Creek. They next appeared in the 1910 census at Watkins, located on the remote plains east of Denver. Ray now worked as a rancher.

All seemed well at Watkins, until it wasn't. In 1911, Jennie was back in Cripple Creek, alone. She might not have appeared on record at all but for one document: weary of the antics of the bawdy women along Myers Avenue, city officials began keeping a register of all female residents in the red-light district. Each woman was asked her birth name, her alias if she had one, her nationality, where she was born and where she most recently came from. Included was a brief description of each woman, and if they left town, it was duly noted when and where they went. Jennie's proportions were small: she was only five feet tall, weighed 106 pounds and had dark skin, brown eyes and black hair. She knew how to read and write. Her date of arrival in town was listed as June 1, 1911. They called her Mexican Jennie.

How did Jennie wind up on the city's register of prostitutes? Because she was living at 447 East Myers Avenue, one of the one-room cribs formerly used by the French girls of the avenue. Jennie is recorded as leaving the district only once. In 1913, she traveled back to Adams County to secure a divorce from Ray Wenner. The divorce was granted on April 13. Her second marriage now just a memory, Jennie soon had a new man in her life. His name was Philip Roberts Jr., and he would prove to be the woman's undoing.

Roberts was a blacksmith at the El Paso Mine and was likely one of Jennie's customers. Even more degrading than being relegated to selling her body for sex was the way Roberts treated Jennie. She would later testify that the man became her pimp, drinking constantly and beating her when she didn't make enough money. It wasn't Jennie's fault—Cripple Creek was slowing down as mining prospects waned, and the city was slowly but surely downsizing. Perhaps to get out from under the nosy officers who cruised Myers Avenue, the couple moved to a small cabin in Poverty Gulch, located roughly one block away just outside of the city limits.

For years, Poverty Gulch was known as a rough neighborhood. A trestle for the Midland Terminal Railroad divided the locale from the city and served as the place where people of color, foreigners, prostitutes, ne'er-do-wells and the rougher element lived. Residents remembered hearing Roberts arguing with Jennie almost nightly. Their last fight took place on Christmas night, 1913, when Roberts threw Jennie to the floor. Jennie pulled a revolver from her trunk and shot the man dead.

Quickly gathering her things, Jennie quietly closed the cabin door and left town as fast as she could. Luck was in her favor, for it would be nearly a week before it occurred to anyone to peek into the silent cabin. There was Roberts, lying stone dead across the blood-soaked bed. The police were summoned, but Jennie was long gone. Roberts's body was shipped to Denver for burial as newspapers got hold of the story. An investigation revealed that several people heard shots being fired around midnight on December 25. Nobody, however, bothered to check on Jennie.

Poverty Gulch was a continuation of Myers Avenue that was conveniently located outside the Cripple Creek City limits. *Courtesy Cripple Creek District Museum.*

The same night Roberts's body was found, a bulletin was sent out to other law enforcement agencies looking for Jennie. Officers in Pueblo arrested a woman named Jennie Tajore who fit Jennie Wenner's description. Her measurements were taken and telegraphed to the police in Cripple Creek, but the woman denied she had ever been to Cripple Creek. Was the woman Jennie? Newspapers did not say, but apparently, she was released on January 3—the same day a Cripple Creek assayer-turned-sheriff named Henry Von Phul decided to go after Mexican Jennie. Because she had once lived in Trinidad and Walsenburg, Von Phul headed south, stopping in Pueblo on the way. There, he discovered that Jennie, alias Juanita Keif, had recently purchased a coach ticket for a southbound train and was headed for Juarez, Mexico.

Had it not been for a delay in train service to Juarez, Von Phul might never have found Jennie. The officer trailed her to El Paso, Texas, where she had bravely swam across the Rio Grande River into Mexico. From there she joined a group of camp followers with a rebel army that was heading to Chihuahua City 250 miles south. What Jennie did not figure on was the determination of Sheriff Von Phul. After poking around in El Paso and Juarez, Von Phul learned of several celebrations going on in Chihuahua City. Within a matter of days, the sheriff appeared there and successfully tracked Jennie down at the Capital Hotel.

It is interesting to note that Jennie is said to have greeted Von Phul warmly and seemed willing to return to Cripple Creek. But the arrest of an American citizen by an American citizen in Mexico proved problematic. Fortunately for Von Phul, General Francisco Villa, better known now as "Pancho" Villa, had just become the governor of Chihuahua. Villa was famous for joining Francisco Madero's uprising against the hated Mexican dictator Porfirio Díaz in 1910. After being caught and sent to a federal military prison in 1912 by General Victoriano Huerta, Villa escaped to the United States. A year later, Madero was assassinated. Villa decided to return to Mexico and formed his own military band. The group staged a revolt against Huerta, and in December of 1913, Villa became governor. It was his group of troops that Jennie had followed to Chihuahua City.

Von Phul was able to meet with Villa and convinced him to order Jennie arrested and incarcerated in the military prison before being transferred to Juarez. But Juarez proved problematic as well. It was there that Von Phul had to bribe a magistrate so he could officially take Jennie into custody. A second issue was the requirement that two American officials were needed to escort American prisoners from Mexico across the border into the United States. Jennie offered to simply walk across the border by herself, but Von Phul had other ideas. He knew that William E. "Billy" Dingman, lately of Cripple Creek, was in the vicinity. In 1912, while working at the Teller County Courthouse, Dingman had stolen a bunch of money and skedaddled. Von Phul found Dingman and made a deal with him: if he would help escort Jennie across the border, Von Phul would "lose" his file. Von Phul must have realized that Jennie's wild story would be of much more interest to newspapers than catching a man who had robbed the county coffers. He was right.

By January 1914, Jennie's story was being splashed all over the newspapers as Von Phul transported her back to Cripple Creek. Nothing was mentioned of Von Phul's deal with Dingman, but there was plenty to say about Jennie. The *Leadville Herald Democrat* claimed that Philip Roberts "was the son of a prominent family here."[177] But the paper also noted that once she crossed the border and was jailed in El Paso, "the little woman occupied a cell at the central police station, spending most of the night in tears" as she denied murdering Roberts and said she wanted to go back to Cripple Creek to clear her name.[178]

When Von Phul and his prisoner arrived in Cripple Creek, the *Herald Democrat* detailed Jennie's confession. She told of how Roberts slapped her before she shot him. When he fell to the floor, the woman "stood over him, firing until the weapon was empty." Curiously, the paper also reported that in her flight, Jennie managed to stop long enough to mail the gun off to New Hampshire. The authorities had somehow retrieved it and showed it to their prisoner. "At the sight of it a half stifled exclamation of surprise came from her," the paper said. According to Jennie's confession, Roberts was holding his own revolver when she shot him. "No I am not sorry," she said, "he would have killed me and not cared."[179]

Jennie's statement conflicted with that of the *Herald Democrat*, which claimed that Cripple Creek police reported Roberts was sleeping peacefully in his bed when he was killed. And two men whom Jennie said she told about the shooting denied knowing anything about it. Her trial began on March 25. It took just two days to convict her as the *Telluride Journal* called the tiny, defenseless woman "one of the most notorious characters in the mining camps of the country."[180] She was sentenced to life imprisonment at the penitentiary in Cañon City in May. With her case closed, Cripple Creek forgot all about Jennie Wenner as she performed the chores and duties assigned to her, including working in the prison sewing room.

It was not until March 1919 that Jennie came back into the public eye. The *Rocky Mountain News* published a sympathetic article about

Mexican Jennie's mug shot from prison shows an angry and ill woman who believed herself innocent of murder. *Courtesy Colorado State Archives.*

her: "One of the really pathetic cases is that of little Jennie Wenner of Cripple Creek, who killed her sweetheart, a young man named Roberts," the paper reported. "According to the matron, Mrs. Kirkham, the girl suffers the pangs of remorse every moment of her waking hours. She refuses to be comforted, and says she would lay down her life any minute if she could only restore the one whose life she took. Jennie is a devout Catholic, and her rosary hangs just above her pillow and the walls of her cell are adorned with religious mottoes and pictures."[181] There was a reason for the article: Jennie was not well, having contracted the dreaded tuberculosis while in prison.

Prison officials considered pardoning Jennie as folks in Cripple Creek rallied for her release. The *Rocky Mountain News* wrote that not only was it generally known that Philip Roberts Jr. "had severely abused" Jennie before she shot him, but also "strong sentiment for her release is said to exist in Teller County."[182] Jennie's case was finally reviewed by the board in 1920. At long last, she walked out of the penitentiary on October

Jennie's beautiful quilt speaks volumes about her life, including the killing of her abuser. *Courtesy of Noelle Rathmell.*

10 a free woman, sold her few belongings to finance a final trip back to Mexico and died in 1924. Three years later, Henry Von Phul died as well. He probably would have liked it that his obituary focused mostly on the case of Mexican Jennie.

The intriguing footnote to Jennie's story lies with the Rocky Mountain Quilt Museum in Golden, which in 1995 exhibited several beautiful handmade quilts from around the state. One of the quilts on display was made by none other than Jennie while she was in prison. Using the fabrics

WICKED CRIPPLE CREEK DISTRICT

at hand, including her own dresses, Jennie carefully pieced her quilt together with intricate stitching, including an embroidered picture of a gun, as well as the figure of Philip Roberts Jr. The quilt was, in its own way, Jennie's autobiography about her life and adventures. Interesting too is the woman who donated the quilt and, in fact, had helped establish the museum by donating one hundred of her own handmade quilts back in 1990. Her name was Eugenia Hartmeister Mitchell.

Mitchell's story was similar to Jennie's: neither of her two husbands were very good to her. When the second one died, Mitchell earned her way by taking in boarders and sewing. Her saving grace was her quilts, which she had been making since she was a child. She loved the patterns and the stories that handmade quilts told. Quite by chance, one of the quilts Mitchell acquired was the one made by Jennie Wenner that had somehow made it to a Colorado antiques dealer.

After years of displaying her quilts at places like the Denver Art Museum and running her own successful quilt store in Golden, Eugenia Mitchell became a founder of the Rocky Mountain Quilt Museum, which opened in 1990. She died in 2006. As for Mexican Jennie's quilt, "Eugenia had loved the quilt so much she never donated it to the museum," wrote poet Barbara Brinson Curiel, whose poem, "Mexican Jenny," won the Philip Levine Prize for Poetry in California in 2012.[183] Even today, the quilt remains in the Mitchell family. "I believe Mexican Jenny's quilt spoke to Eugenia Mitchell," Curiel wrote, "as it spoke to me: because of its testimony to a woman's determination to tell her own story under the most difficult circumstances and in an environment where these stories are silenced."[184]

NEW GAMBLING IN AN OLD TOWN

For over forty years beginning in 1948, Cripple Creek and Victor—the only two official populated cities left in the Cripple Creek District—figured out how to make the most of what they had left in the shops, restaurants, bars and hotels. There was the Cripple Creek Inn, the first tavern in Teller County to purchase a liquor license when Prohibition was repealed in 1933. In Victor, Zeke's Place was a local favorite where cocktails and food were served by two generations of the Yeager family. The 1896 Imperial Hotel had been purchased by Wayne and Dorothy Mackin, who not only upped the game for fine dining and hotel stays but also began hosting highly popular melodrama shows. Today the melodrama is still performed but at the Butte Theater, an original opera house that has been restored.

Throughout the 1950s and '60s, new stores, restaurants and bars began filling the old buildings in Cripple Creek and Victor. Within a few short years the Cripple Creek District Museum, the Cripple Creek & Victor Narrow Gauge Railroad, the Mollie Kathleen Mine, the Old Homestead House Museum, the Victor Lowell Thomas Museum and a host of other history-minded attractions opened for business. There were also several ghost towns to explore. But that was in the days before mining was renewed, destroying most of the ghost towns and even whole mountains in a new quest to find gold. Today only a few remnants of the old mines and mills are left, but they are very much worth seeing.

On a much quieter level, gambling remained alive and well in the district for years. The tradition of illegal gambling continued well into the 1940s with speakeasies in places like the basement of the Victor Elks Lodge, open slot machines at the Cripple Creek Elks Lodge and back rooms of taverns like the Cripple Creek Inn and other places. But in 1951, a group of reporters from Denver happened to visit Teller County and were accordingly treated to all the outlawed games of chance. Unfortunately, the group returned to Denver and blabbed about what they had seen and done. Within a short time, gambling raids were staged all over Teller County, and the second era of gaming in the district came to an end. The third era began in November 1990, when voters supported legalized gambling in Cripple Creek, Central City and Black Hawk. The highest stake was set at five dollars.

Over the next year, the ghosts of Cripple Creek awoke to the sounds of their old haunts being transformed into new casinos. Real estate prices went through the roof. Campaign literature had explained that of the gaming proceeds in Cripple Creek, as well as Central City and Black

Some of Cripple Creek's famous donkey herd is seen here in front of the Cripple Creek District Museum during the annual Donkey Derby Days celebration. *Author's collection.*

Today the Victor Lowell Thomas Museum has displays about the famed radio host, as well as the city's illustrious past. *Author's collection.*

Hawk, 50 percent would go to the Colorado General Fund, with another 28 percent providing Historic Preservation funding statewide. Teller and Gilpin Counties would net 12 percent, with the last 10 percent being distributed among the three gaming cities. That meant higher wages than most businesses across Colorado were paying, and employees willing to commute to or live in these towns made big money in the way of hourly pay, salaries and tips.

As gambling premiered on October 1, 1991, Bennett Avenue came alive once again with people, music, events, and lots of fun. With all the free coupons flying around, it was said that a person could walk up one end of Bennett and down the other getting free coin, free meals and free drinks and still come out ahead without ever touching a slot machine. Several casinos offered players clubs with big payouts for points. But Cripple Creek was not just a gambler's paradise. There were hundreds of jobs: bartender, card dealer, cashier, chef, cook, hotel staff, maintenance worker, manager, players club staff, security worker, slot technician, waiter or any number of other positions available. In the infant days of gaming, it was not uncommon for a customer to tip 10 percent or more following a big win. But it wasn't long before certain people in the gaming community wanted more.

Stories began floating around about how certain cocktail waitresses and other employees would flock to a player who hit a jackpot, hoping to mooch a tip from the winnings. An amateur slot player might hit a jackpot and, thinking they had somehow broken the device, get up and wander away as someone else stepped in and claimed the winnings. It wasn't unusual to find money sitting in the payout trays or lying on the floor, even though gaming laws prohibited customers and employees from scooping it up. A favorite among veteran gamblers was the cup underneath the bar-top poker machines that caught coins when the machine malfunctioned or the wrong denomination was fed into the slot. It was easy to surreptitiously reach under the bar and retrieve the money from the cup without being spotted by the security cameras (today, most of Cripple Creek's slots use the ticket-in-ticket-out system to play or cash in their winnings, called TITO for short. Some servers who miss the cash tips of the old days joke that TITO really stands for "Tipping is totally optional.").

Some employees went to even further extents to reap illegal money from their places of employment. In 1993, for instance, an armed man appeared at the cashier window of what was then the Gold Rush Casino

The Gold Rush Casino as it looked when it was robbed at gunpoint. *Author's collection.*

and demanded money. He received around $7,900 in cash and ordered a nearby cashier to put it in a bag. Once the bag was filled, the robber dragged the cashier out of a side door of the casino at gunpoint and disappeared. But when a security guard peeked out of the door to see where the thief went, he watched as the kidnap victim ran around to the driver's side of a car in the parking lot and drove off. Police later found the hysterical cashier, alone, on remote Shelf Road leading to Cañon City. Officers remained suspicious and raided a Cañon City apartment the next morning. There sat the cashier, her robber husband and a third accomplice with the stolen money in a pile on the coffee table. All three were arrested, tried for the robbery and sentenced to jail.

Another time, it was discovered that a player's club associate at another casino had created an account with a fake name, gradually added points to the account and cashed them out to the tune of over $100,000. The last big heist took place in 2003 when, in the early morning hours, a man entered J.P. McGills Casino. He was wearing a coat and hat and was able to easily access the vault, where he stole an amazing $300,000. He encountered only one employee on his way out the door, to whom he gave a casual nod before leaving and disappearing into the night. It took a year before investigators finally caught the suspect.

Part of the district's gold boom today can be found in collectible casino tokens from over thirty years of legal gambling. *Author's collection.*

The occasional crime aside, the Cripple Creek District today thrives not just because of the casinos but also numerous events, attractions, camping, fishing, hiking trails, historic hotels, museums, restaurants, saloons, shops, restaurants and a variety of scenic drives. Still in place are decades-old celebrations like Donkey Derby Days in Cripple Creek and Gold Rush Days in Victor. Cripple Creek promotes its history and its casinos, while Victor and the bedroom community of Goldfield survive as two of the last authentic gold rush towns in the West with lots of history to explore. The district remains as one of the most historic places in America even today, its past riddled with deliciously wicked history that will be remembered for decades to come.

NOTES

Introduction

1. Jan MacKell Collins, "Winfield Scott Stratton, Colorado's Mystifying Millionaire," https://janmackellcollins.wordpress.com.

Chapter 1. Cripple Creek's First Murder Victim

2. Castle Rock Journal, December 12, 1883.
3. *Rocky Mountain News*, April 1, 1892.
4. Ibid., April 3, 1892.
5. *Pueblo Daily Chieftain*, April 3, 1892.
6. *Aspen Daily Chronicle*, April 2, 1892.
7. Ibid.; *Rocky Mountain News*, April 3, 1892.
8. *Pueblo Daily Chieftain*, April 3, 1892.
9. *Rocky Mountain News*, April 3, 1892.
10. *Pueblo Daily Chieftain*, April 3, 1892.
11. *Rocky Mountain News*, April 3, 1892.
12. Ibid., April 25, 1892.
13. *Svensk-Amerikanska Western* (translated), April 28, 1892.
14. According to the Pikes Peak Genealogical Society, Mount Pisgah's earliest marked burial is James Gozad, who died in May of 1892. The cemetery would become an official burial ground in 1895. Tombstone Inscriptions of Teller County, Mount Pisgah Cemetery, Pikes Peak Genealogical Society, https://tombstone-inscriptions.ppgs.org.
15. *Rocky Mountain News*, May 8, 1892.

Chapter 2. The Heist at the Hotel Victor

16. *Cripple Creek Morning Journal*, September 28, 1894.
17. Ibid., October 4, 1894.
18. Ibid., October 13, 1894.
19. *Rocky Mountain News*, October 15, 1894.
20. *Cripple Creek Morning Journal*, October 16, 1894.
21. Ibid.

Chapter 3. The Killing of Richard Newell

22. Pueblo *Daily Chieftain*, January 27, 1893, 1.
23. Robinson, *Colorado Reports*, 59–67.
24. Ibid.
25. Ibid.
26. Ibid.
27. *Colorado Springs Weekly Gazette*, January 3, 1895.
28. *Walsenburg World*, June 5, 1895.

Chapter 4. The Robbery of the Florence and Cripple Creek Train

29. *Phillips County (MT) Herald*, March 29, 1895.
30. Newspapers constantly misspelled Louis Vanneck's name. They never did get it right.
31. Author Marshall Sprague claimed that Taylor's sister, Nell, was once married to Sherman Crumley. There is no official record of such a union, however, leading to speculation that the marriage was of the common law variety (Sprague, *Money Mountain*, 202).
32. *Rocky Mountain News*, July 24, 1895.
33. *Colorado Daily Chieftain*, July 25, 1895.
34. *Rocky Mountain News*, July 25, 1895.
35. *Cañon City Daily Record*, September 5, 1907.

Chapter 5. Officers Down: Fallen Lawmen of the District

36. Colorado State Patrol, "Officer E.T. Clark," Colorado Fallen Hero Biographies, https://csp.colorado.gov; Officer Down Memorial Page, "Patrolman Elim T. Clark," www.odmp.org.
37. *Aspen Democrat*, September 23, 2022, 1.

38. *Rocky Mountain News*, September 22, 1902.
39. For the story of Leabo and Miller's deaths, see chapter 5.
40. *Leadville Herald Democrat*, November 11, 1908.
41. *Wet Mountain Tribune*, November 14, 1908.
42. Officer Down Memorial Page, "Night Marshal Harvey Calvin 'Cal' Neese," www.odmp.org; *Fort Collins Courier*, July 3, 1920.
43. *Rocky Mountain News*, July 4, 1920.
44. Find a Grave, "Morris William Dolan," findagrave.com.
45. Ibid.
46. Miscellaneous clipping, author's files.

Chapter 6. Countess Douglas McPherson

47. *Victor Record*, July 27, 1898.
48. Ibid., August 23, 1898.
49. Boag, *Re-Dressing America's Frontier Past*, 79–80.
50. Jameson, *All That Glitters*, 39.
51. *Cripple Creek Daily Press*, July 26, 1901. Author Peter Boag pondered whether Billy Mercer and Billy Millar were one and the same person (Boag, *Re-Dressing America's Frontier Past*, 79–80).

Chapter 7. The Harlot Who Burned Down Cripple Creek

52. Collins, *Lost Ghost Towns*, 71.
53. Library of Congress, 1893 Cripple Creek/Fremont Sanborn Fire Insurance Map, www.loc.gov.
54. *Cripple Creek Morning Journal*, November 11, 1894.
55. *Leadville Herald Democrat*, November 16, 1898.
56. *Rocky Mountain News*, April 30, 1896.
57. *Boulder Daily Camera*, April 29, 1896.

Chapter 8. The Hole in the Wall Gang's Hideout

58. Interview with Bob Lee by William A. Pinkerton, Pinkerton Detective Agency, May 5, 1900, Hadsell Collection, Wyoming State Archives.
59. Lamb, *Kid Curry*, 124. The story of Bob Lee in Cripple Creek is best told by Lamb, whose family in Colorado knew Harvey Logan. During the winter of 1903–4, before he was killed following his last train robbery near the town of Parachute near Grand Junction, Logan told of the Hole in the Wall Gang's escapades

to the Lambs. Understandably, the book was written years later, and Lamb's recollections of exactly when certain events took place were a little muddled. Wherever possible, historical archives, newspaper accounts, city directories and Sanborn Fire Insurance maps have been used to corroborate Lamb's memories.

60. Ibid., 124.

61. Ibid., 127.

62. Record of interview with Bob Lee by John C. Fraser, Pinkerton Report, June 7, 1900, Frank Hadsell Papers, Research Collection H 70-18, Wyoming State Archives and Historical Department, Cheyenne, Wyoming.

63. Ibid.

64. Record of jewelry items taken at the Wilcox Robbery June 2, 1899, Hadsell Collection, Wyoming State Archives; Van Ryzin, "Bank Notes Forever Tied."

65. Notably, several writers have made valid attempts to verify when, how and where Bob Lee and Lonnie Logan were in the months following the Wilcox Robbery. Their hard research aside, it is best to go by the original testimony of Bob Lee after he was arrested in early 1901. Record of interview with Bob Lee by William A. Pinkerton.

66. Author Brown Waller wrote that Lonnie and Bob were still in Harlem when the Pinkertons arrived but managed to escape out of the back door of the Club Saloon, made their way to Zurich Water Tank west of Harlem and boarded a westbound Great Northern Train (Waller, *Last of the Great*, 136–37).

67. *Phillips County (MT) News*, January 17, 1900.

68. Lamb, *Kid Curry*, 77–78.

69. Letter to Frank Hadsell, U.S. Marshall, Cheyenne Wyoming, from James McParland, Asst. Genl. Supt. W.D., Pinkerton's, July 30, 1900, Hadsell Collection, Wyoming State Archives.

70. *Cripple Creek Morning Times-Citizen*, March 1, 1900.

71. Ibid.

72. Lamb, *Kid Curry*, 213.

73. Interview with Bob Lee by William A. Pinkerton.

74. News clipping, *Cheyenne Leader*, Monday May 28, 1900, Wyoming State Archives.

75. Letters to Frank Hadsell, U.S. Marshall, Cheyenne Wyoming, from Frank Murray, Pinkerton National Detective Agency, dated June 8 and June 14, 1900, Hadsell Collection, Wyoming State Archives.

76. Letter to U.S. District Attorney T.F. Burke, Cheyenne, Wyoming, from James McParland, Assistant General Superintendent, Pinkerton's National Detective Agency, July 20, 1900, Hadsell Collection, Wyoming State Archives.

77. Letter to Frank Hadsell, from G.J. Spencer of Station D., S. St. Joseph, Missouri dated February 16, 1901, Hadsell Collection, Wyoming State Archives.

78. Letter to Frank Hadsell, U.S. Marshal, Cheyenne Wyoming from Robert E. Lee, Wyoming State Penitentiary at Rawlins dated February 2,1902, Hadsell Collection, Wyoming State Archives.

Chapter 9. Teddy Roosevelt's Problem Child

79. *Cripple Creek Morning Times*, May 17, 1898.
80. *Dodge City Globe*, March 16, 1886.
81. Miller and Snett, "Some Notes on Kansas Cowtown," 204–205.
82. *Bent County Register*, January 29, 1887, 3.
83. The towns of Cimarron and Ingalls were battling over the county seat. Bill Tilghman, Daniels and other lawmen had tried to take the records from Cimarron. A six-hour gun battle ensued but nothing was settled in the end (Patterson, *Historical Atlas of the Outlaw West*, 64).
84. *Rocky Mountain News*, April 10, 1891; DeArment, *Gunfighter in Gotham*, 40–41.
85. *Rocky Mountain News*, May 17, 1892, 2.
86. MacKell, "Crooked Poker Table."
87. *Cripple Creek Morning Times*, May 17, 1898.
88. MacKell, "Crooked Poker Table."
89. *Cripple Creek Morning Times*, July 31, 1898.
90. *Durango Democrat*, January 16, 1902.
91. MacKell, "Crooked Poker Table."
92. MacKell, "'Monument to a Damned Fool," 10.
93. Ibid.

Chapter 10. The Vixen Who Burned Down Victor

94. *Victor Record*, May 5, 1898.
95. Ibid., July 29, 1899, 5.
96. Other sources say the woman was named Lily Reid, or Rosa May, also that some folks were smoking opium and accidentally knocked over a lamp. But since the *Victor Record* was literally located closest to the incident, its story is likely most accurate.
97. *Victor Record*, August 22, 1899.
98. Ibid.
99. Ibid., August 31, 1899.

Chapter 11. Joe Moore and a Deadly Parade

100. *Cripple Creek Morning Journal*, December 22, 1894; *Cripple Creek Morning Times*, January 26, 1898; *Victor Record*, August 19, 1898; *Cripple Creek Morning Journal*, April 13, 1895.
101. *Victor Record*, March 9, 1899.
102. Ibid.
103. *Cripple Creek Morning Times*, March 12, 1899.
104. Ibid.
105. *Victor Daily Record*, June 8, 1899.

Chapter 12. To Tease a Dying Man

106. *Rocky Mountain News*, January 30, 1901.
107. Bell, "Surreptitiously Sawed Off Dead Man's Skull," undated news clipping, Cripple Creek District Museum archives, Cripple Creek, Colorado.
108. *Rocky Mountain News*, December 26, 1901.
109. Ibid.
110. *Leadville Herald Democrat*, December 26, 1901.
111. Bell, "Surreptitiously Sawed Off Dead Man's Skull."
112. *Rocky Mountain News*, December 26, 1901, and December 27, 1901.
113. Ibid., March 9, 1902.
114. Bell, "Surreptitiously Sawed Off Dead Man's Skull"
115. Ibid.
116. History Blog, "'Eggshell Skull' Moves."

Chapter 13. The Plight of Pyromaniac Roy Bourquin

117. *Washington (KS) Weekly Post*, March 2, 1887.
118. *Washington (KS) Republican*, June 1, 1894.
119. Asylum Projects, "Colorado State Industrial."
120. *Victor Record*, May 1, 1900.
121. *Rocky Mountain News*, June 16, 1902.
122. Ibid., May 18, 1905.
123. Ibid., July 16, 1905.
124. *San Juan Prospector*, March 30, 1907.
125. Ibid.
126. *Rocky Mountain News*, March 30, 1907.
127. Ancestry, "U.S., Civil War Pension Index."

128. *Independence (KS) Daily Reporter*, December 29, 1913.

129. Ancestry, "World War I Draft Registrations."

130. *Evening Vanguard* (Venice, CA), January 8, 1952.

Chapter 14. Redemption for the Crumleys

131. *Rocky Mountain News*, June 23, 1894.

132. Writer Fred Huston appears to have been one of the first to claim that the Crumley brothers were mixed up with the notorious Dalton Gang, who later met their end in Coffeyville, Kansas, in 1892 (Huston, "Showdown at Cripple Creek," 20).

133. *Cripple Creek Morning Times*, August 20, 1898, and August 23, 1898.

134. *Victor Record*, April 4, 1901.

135. For the full story of Eliza Jane "Lida" Crumley, see Collins, *Wild Women of Prescott*.

136. Sprague, *Money Mountain*, 225.

137. Ibid.

138. *Victor Record*, August 23, 1901.

139. Sprague, *Money Mountain*, 226.

140. *Victor Record*, August 23, 1901.

141. *Morning Appeal* (Carson City, NV), June 4, 1904.

142. *Tonopah Daily Bonanza*, December 28, 1907.

143. Ibid., January 1, 1908.

144. Ibid., May 2, 1909.

145. Ibid., September 4, 1910, and September 19, 1910, 1.

146. Ibid., May 23, 1911, 1.

147. Brian Tim Wellesley, Reno, Nevada, correspondence with the author, 1999–2001.

148. Email correspondence with Helen (last name unknown), who knew the Crumley family, by author, 1999.

Chapter 15. The Most Hated Man in the Cripple Creek District

149. *Rocky Mountain News*, November 12, 1897.

150. Find a Grave, "James A 'Jim Lambert' Warford," findagrave.com.

151. *Colorado Springs Weekly Gazette*, November 10, 1904.

152. *Rocky Mountain News*, April 21, 1912.

153. *Lead (SD) Daily Call*, April 20, 1912.

154. *Daily Deadwood Pioneer-Times*, April 20, 1912.

Chapter 16. The Story of a Murdered Mistress

155. Langdon, *Cripple Creek Strike*, 324.
156. *Boulder Daily Camera*, April 13, 1905.
157. *Florence Daily Tribune*, April 13, 1905.
158. *Rocky Mountain News*, April 14, 1905.
159. Ibid.
160. *Colorado Springs Gazette Telegraph*, February 6, 1905.
161. *Rocky Mountain News*, April 14, 1905.
162. Ibid.
163. *Leadville Herald Democrat*, April 14, 1905.
164. Ibid.
165. *Rocky Mountain News*, April 14, 1905.
166. *Florence Daily Tribune*, April 13, 1905.
167. *Rocky Mountain News*, April 14, 1905.
168. Ibid.
169. Ibid., April 15, 1905.

Chapter 17. "Pretty Jack" McEachern, the Body Snatcher

170. *Leadville Herald Democrat*, February 12, 1906.
171. *Rocky Mountain News*, February 11, 1906,
172. Leadville *Herald Democrat*, March 8, 1906.
173. *Rocky Mountain News*, March 14, 1906.
174. Ibid., March 23, 1906.
175. *San Miguel Examiner* (Telluride, CO), June 21, 1919.

Chapter 18. Mexican Jennie: A Quilted Autobiography

176. Brinson Curiel, *Mexican Jenny*, 27–28.
177. Leadville *Herald Democrat*, January 24, 1914.
178. Ibid., January 25, 1914.
179. Ibid., February 1, 1914.
180. *Telluride Journal* 33, no. 39 (April 1914): 3.
181. *Rocky Mountain News*, March 30, 1919.
182. Ibid., February 20, 1920.
183. Brinson Curiel, "Poet in the Archive," unpublished essay provided to the author.
184. Ibid.

BIBLIOGRAPHY

Archives

Cripple Creek District Directories, 1894–1918, Cripple Creek District Museum, Cripple Creek, Colorado.

Cripple Creek Mortuary Records, Cripple Creek District Museum, Cripple Creek, Colorado.

Jones, Shirley Farris. "Harvey Calvin Neese: From Coffee County TN to Cripple Creek CO," Privately published, 2010, Cripple Creek District Museum archives, Cripple Creek, Colorado.

Articles

Bell, Jack. "Surreptitiously Sawed Off Dead Man's Skull to Use It in Defending Man Who Killed Him." *Denver Post*, n.d.

Bommersbach, Jana. "Homos on the Range." *True West*, November 1, 2005. https://truewestmagazine.com.

Brinson Curiel, Barbara. "A Poet in the Archive: Writing Chicana History." July 2023.

Gibbard, Frank. "Gunfight at the Polls: The James Warford Murder Trials." *Colorado Lawyer* 49, no. 11 (December 2020): 20. https://law-journals-books.vlex.com.

Huston, Fred. "Showdown at Cripple Creek." *Frontier West*, February 1974.

MacKell, Jan. "A Crooked Poker Table, Teddy's Rough Riders and the Life of Ben Daniels." *Colorado Gambler*, December 2006.

————. "'Monument to a Damned Fool or, What Really Happened to Finn's Folly." *Colorado Gambler*, 2002.

Miller, Nyle H., and Joseph W. Snett. "Some Notes on Kansas Cowtown Police Officers and Gun Fighters." *Kansas Historical Quarterly* 26 (1960): 204–5.

Books

Alexander Leggett, Ann, and Jordan Alexander Leggett. *Ghosts of Boulder*. Charleston, SC: Arcadia Publishing, 2013.

Bauer, William H., James L. Ozment and John H. Willard. *Colorado Post Offices, 1859–1989*. Golden, CO: Colorado Railroad Historical Foundation, 1990.

Blewer, Mac. *Wyoming's Outlaw Trail*. Charleston, SC: Arcadia Publishing, 2013.

Boag, Peter. *Re-Dressing America's Frontier Past*. Los Angeles: University of California Press, 2011.

Brinson Curiel, Barbara. *Mexican Jenny and Other Poems*. Tallahassee, FL: Anhinga Press, 2014.

Brown, Robert L. *Colorado Ghost Towns*. Caldwell, ID: Caxton Printers, 1972.

————. *Ghost Towns of the Colorado Rockies*. Caldwell, ID: Caxton Printers, 1968.

Collins, Jan Mackell. *Good Time Girls of Colorado: A Red-Light History of the Centennial State*. Lanham, MD: Rowman & Littlefield Publishing Group, 2019.

————. *Good Time Girls of Nevada and Utah: A Red-Light History of the American West*. Lanham, MD: Rowman & Littlefield Publishing Group, 2022.

————. *Lost Ghost Towns of Teller County* Charleston, SC: The History Press, 2016.

————. *Wild Women of Prescott, Arizona*. Charleston, SC: The History Press, 2015.

Cullen, Frank, Florence Hackman and Donald McNeilly. *Vaudeville Old and New: An Encyclopedia of Variety Performances in America*. Boca Raton, FL: Psychology Press, a division of Routledge, 2007.

DeArment, Robert K. *Gunfighter in Gotham: Bat Masterson's New York City Years*. Norman: University of Oklahoma Press, 2013.

Emrich, David. *Hollywood, Colorado*. Lakewood, CO: Post Modern Company, 1997.

Feitz, Leland. *Cripple Creek Railroads*. Colorado Springs, CO: Little London Press, 1968.

————. *Victor, A Quick History*. Colorado Springs, CO: Little London Press, 1969.

Horan, James D. *The Pinkertons: The Detective Dynasty That Made History*. New York: Crown Publishing Group, 1967.

Jameson, Elizabeth. *All That Glitters: Class, Conflict and Community in Cripple Creek*. Urbana and Chicago: University of Illinois Press, 1998.

Karp, Larry. *Brun Campbell: The Original Ragtime Kid*. Jefferson, NC: McFarland & Co., 2016.

Kelly, Charles. *The Outlaw Trail: The Story of Butch Cassidy and the Hole in the Wall Gang.* New York: Bonanza Books, 1938.

Lamb, F. Bruce. *Kid Curry: The Life and Times of Harvey Logan and the Hole in the Wall Gang.* Boulder, CO: Johnson Books, 1991.

Langdon, Emma. *The Cripple Creek Strike: A History of Industrial Wars in Colorado 1903-4-5.* Denver, CO: Great Western Publishing Company, 1905.

Levine, Brian. *Cripple Creek: City of Influence.* Cripple Creek, CO: City of Cripple Creek, 1994.

MacKell, Jan. *Brothels, Bordellos & Bad Girls: Prostitution in Colorado 1860 to 1930.* Albuquerque, NM: University of New Mexico Press, 2003.

————. *Cripple Creek District: Last of Colorado's Gold Booms.* Charleston, SC: Arcadia Publishing, 2003.

Mazzulla, Fred, and Jo Mazzulla. *The First 100 Years: Cripple Creek and the Pikes Peak Region.* Denver, CO: A.B. Hirschfeld Press, 1968.

McFarland, Edward M. *The Cripple Creek Road.* Boulder, CO: Pruett Publishing, 1984.

Patterson, Richard M. *Historical Atlas of the Outlaw West.* Boulder, CO: Johnson Books, 2007.

Pointer, Larry. *In Search of Butch Cassidy.* Oklahoma City: University of Oklahoma Press, 1977.

Robinson, T.M. *Colorado Reports: Cases Adjudged in the Supreme Court of Colorado at the September, 1895, January and April Terms, 1896.* Vol. 22. New York: Banks and Brothers Law Publishers, 1897.

Sprague, Marshall. *Money Mountain: The Story of Cripple Creek Gold.* Lincoln: University of Nebraska Press, 1979.

Waller, Brown. *Last of the Great Western Train Robbers.* South Brunswick, NJ: A.S. Barnes, 1968.

Internet

Allen, Tommy. "The Hotel Victor Robbery of 1894." *Stories from the Midland,* www.storiesfromthemidland.com.

American Federation of Labor and Congress of Industrial Organizations, "The Battle of Cripple Creek," https://aflcio.org/about/history/labor-history-events/battle-cripple-creek.

Ancestry.com.

Asylum Projects. "Colorado State Industrial School for Boys." www.asylumprojects.org.

Brodrick, Sean. "Colorado Gold Rush." Weiss Ratings Daily, September 18, 2018, https://weissratings.com.

Brown, Andrea. "Skull Finally Finds a Home, but Where's the Body?" *Colorado Springs Gazette*, April 27, 2010, https://gazette.com.

Bureau of Land Management GLO Records, https://glorecords.blm.gov.

City of Victor. https://www.victorcolorado.com/history.htm.

Collins, Jan MacKell. "Goldfield History." Western Mining History. https://westernmininghistory.com.

———. "The Untold Truth About LGBTQ+ People In The Wild West." Grunge, January 31, 2023. www.grunge.com.

———. "Victor." *Colorado Encyclopedia*. https://coloradoencyclopedia.org.

Colorado Encyclopedia. "Cotopaxi Train Robbery." https://coloradoencyclopedia.org.

Colorado Historic Newspapers Collection. https://www.coloradohistoricnewspapers.org.

Colorado State Capitol. "Dome Restoration." https://capitol.colorado.gov/projects/dome-restoration.

Cripple Creek District Museum. "District Museum Cures Winter Blues!" http://www.cripplecreekrailroads.com.

Daviess County Historical Society. "Mining War Gunfighter Jim Warford (alias Jim Lambert)." https://daviesscountyhistoricalsociety.com.

Everything Elko. "Elko County Sesquicentennial 1869–2019." https://everythingelko.com.

Flores, Devin. "1904: The Most Corrupt Election in Colorado History." History Colorado, September 30, 2020. https://www.historycolorado.org.

Geller, J.L., J. Erlen and R.L. Pinkus. "A Historical Appraisal of America's Experience with 'Pyromania'—A Diagnosis in Search of a Disorder." National Library of Medicine, 1986. https://pubmed.ncbi.nlm.nih.gov/3542858.

Goldfield Historical Society. "Goldfield Nevada." Walking tour booklet, 2013. http://goldfieldhistoricalsociety.com.

Gross, Ben. "A Truly Amazing Broadcaster." Magazine clipping, CIA government reading room, https://www.cia.gov.

The History Blog. "Eggshell Skull' Moves from Courthouse to Museum." www.thehistoryblog.com.

Howard Hickson's Histories. "Is Everybody Happy?" https://www.gbcnv.edu.

Internet Movie Database. www.imdb.com.

"Jack Bell (1864–1952): Miner, Newspaperman and Naturalist." https://www.iment.com/maida/family/father/jackbell/jackbelltimeline.htm.

Martin, Claire. "Quilts Told Story of Eugenia Mitchell's Life." *Denver Post*, December 22, 2006, https://www.denverpost.com.

Medical News Today. "Pyromaniac: What It Means, Symptoms, and More." https://www.medicalnewstoday.com.

National Register of Historic Places. Nomination for the Victor Hotel. https://npgallery.nps.gov.

Newspapers.com.

Nowakowski, Konrad. "Brun Campbell: Notes on His Early Life and Unknown Pictures." Syncopated Times: Exploring the World of Hot Jazz, Ragtime and Swing, October 29, 2020. https://syncopatedtimes.com.

Pueblo County Insane Asylum. https://www.kmitch.com/Pueblo/asylumb.html.

Summers, Danny. "From the Sidelines: A Bullfight? You Bet!" *The Tribune* (Colorado), August 7, 2019. https://gazette.com.

Van Ryzin, Robert R. "Bank Notes Forever Tied to Wild Bunch." NumismaticNews, May 16, 2016. https://www.numismaticnews.net.

Western Mining History. https://westernmininghistory.com.

WikiTree. "Robert Earnest Lewis." https://www.wikitree.com.

World History. "Wild Bunch—The Wilcox Robbery: Who Did It?" https://worldhistory.us.

Interviews

Brinson Curiel, Barbara. Interview by the author, 2023.

Hack, Henry "June," and Margaret Hack. Interview by the author, Cripple Creek, Colorado, 1997.

Hern, Harold. Interview by the author, Cripple Creek, Colorado, 2001.

Hilliard, Stephanie. Interview by the author, Victor, Colorado, 2002.

Keller, James E. Victor mayor. Interview by the author, Victor, Colorado, 1992.

Smith, Eleanor. Interview by the author, Colorado City, Colorado, 1997.

Swanson, Erik. Director of the Cripple Creek District Museum. Interviews by the author, 1998–2005.

Tremayne, Loretta Bielz. Interview by the author, Cripple Creek, 1997.

Trenary, Melissa Mueller. Interviews by the author, 2019–2022.

Twitty, Eric. Interview by the author, Victor, Colorado, 1999.

Manuscripts

"Florence R.R. History." Unpublished manuscript, date and author unknown. Collection of Jan MacKell Collins.

BIBLIOGRAPHY

Newspapers

ARIZONA
Arizona Republic
Bisbee Daily Review

CALIFORNIA
Evening Vanguard
Los Angeles Herald

CANADA
Ontario St. Catherines Standard

COLORADO
Akron Weekly Pioneer Press
Aspen Daily Chronicle
Aspen Daily Times
Aspen Morning Sun
Bent County Register
Boulder Daily Camera
Cañon City Daily Record
Cañon City Record
Castle Rock Journal
Colorado Democrat
Colorado Springs Gazette
Colorado Springs Gazette Telegraph
Colorado Springs Weekly Gazette
Colorado Statesman
Colorado Transcript
Cripple Creek Daily Press
Cripple Creek Gold Rush
Cripple Creek Morning Journal
Cripple Creek Morning Times
Denver United Labor Bulletin
Durango Democrat
Durango Semi-Weekly Herald
Florence Daily Tribune
Gilpin Observer
Grand Junction Daily Sentinel

Greeley Tribune
Holyoke Phillips County Herald
Holyoke State Herald
Idaho Springs Mining Gazette
Idaho Springs News
Idaho Springs Siftings-News
Lafayette News
Lamar Register
Larimer County Independent
Leadville Herald Democrat
Longmont Daily Times
Longmont Times-Call
Meeker Herald
Montrose Daily Press
Oak Creek Times
Pueblo Courier
Pueblo Daily Chieftain
Rocky Ford Enterprise
Rocky Mountain News
Salida Mail
San Juan Prospector
San Miguel Examiner
Silver Cliff Rustler
Svensk-Amerikanska Western
Telluride Journal
Trinidad Chronicle-News
Victor Record
Walsenburg World
Wet Mountain Tribune

GEORGIA
Atlanta Constitution

KANSAS
Dodge City Globe
Dodge City Journal-Democrat
Dodge City Sun

Washington County Post
Washington Republican

MINNESOTA
St. Paul Daily Globe

MONTANA
Harlem Enterprise
Helena Independent
Phillips County News

NEBRASKA
Omaha Evening Bee

NEVADA
Carson City Nevada Morning Appeal
Elko Weekly Independent
Goldfield News
Tonopah Bonanza
Tonopah Daily Bonanza

NEW MEXICO
Santa Fe Daily New Mexican

NEW YORK
Buffalo Enquirer
New York Times
Rochester Democrat and Chronicle

OHIO
Lima Times-Democrat
Mansfield News-Journal

PENNSYLVANIA
Philadelphia Inquirer
Pittsburgh Press

SOUTH DAKOTA
Daily Deadwood Pioneer-Times

Deadwood Evening Independent
Lead Daily Call

TEXAS
El Paso Times

UTAH
Price Sun-Advocate
Salt Lake City Herald

VIRGINIA
Richmond Palladium-Item

WASHINGTON
Seattle Post-Intelligencer

WEST VIRGINIA
Martinsburg Herald

WYOMING
Cheyenne Leader
Wyoming Tribune

ABOUT THE AUTHOR

*J*an MacKell Collins has been rambling around the West for most of her life, taking copious notes and photographs about the people, places and events that were integral to shaping the American West. A former longtime resident of the Cripple Creek District, she has been a published author and speaker since 2003, with a devout fondness for the wicked side of history. Her work has also appeared in numerous local and regional periodicals for nearly three decades. Ms. Collins currently resides in the East, where she continues her research and writings under the tender mollycoddling of two spoiled cats, an equally spoiled dog and her ever patient husband.

Visit us at
www.historypress.com